200 Years

YONGE

A History

Contents

INTRODUCTION

Photo by Ian Davenport

In 1996 the communities along Yonge Street celebrated the bicentennial of this historic Canadian thoroughfare. It was advertised by the media as a celebration of the 200th anniversary of the longest street in the world (i.e. from Lake Ontario to Rainy River). But the Yonge Street we celebrated was that conceived by Lieutenant-Governor John Graves Simcoe in the years prior to 1796. This was Simcoe's military road, the long portage, along the Don River, between Lake Ontario and Lake Simcoe, the ancient path of the First Nations people who travelled it from time immemorial. Then, and now, it opens all of Central Ontario to travel and commerce.

The historical societies and organizations serving the communities of Toronto, York Region, and Simcoe County, under the guidance of Jane Beecroft of the Community History Project (CHP) of Toronto, generated a series of 2 by 3-ft. panels depicting their unique perspectives of Yonge Street history. Some 68 boards were produced and displayed at Toronto and York Region malls during 1996. These were also part of the many community celebrations that year. Afterwards, the Greater Metro Heritage Group released them to the Newmarket Historical Society for display in the Region of York Administrative Building on Yonge Street in Newmarket, where they remained on show in the rotunda of this building after 1996. The public attention they generated prompted the then Regional Chair Eldred King and Information Officer John Scott to decide it would be appropriate for the Region to publish a book based on this material, since York was about to assume jurisdiction over Yonge Street from the Province of Ontario.

That is where my relationship with the book began. As the creator of these displays for the history of Newmarket, I was soon in contact with the *200 years YONGE* committees of the historical societies of Richmond Hill, Aurora, East Gwillimbury, Bradford and Innisfil, each of whom cooperated in making their records available. Later, with the assistance of many people, I became involved in transforming the panel materials into electronic files for publication. My close friend, and historical and computer cohort, Paul Millard of the Newmarket Historical Society, helped me scan the many pictures and sketches in the original material in preparation for production. Jane Beecroft was instrumental in securing the original print materials from the Ontario Genealogical Society, which had retained this data on computer disk, thus saving many hours of composition and retyping.

To round out the total picture of what Yonge Street was and had become, we thought it would be appropriate to add some extra elements to the collection of historical panels. I had photographed many of the events associated with the 1996 celebrations. As well, I had a selection of photos from a set of 70, taken at various Yonge Street locations in 1922 by Alexander Galbraith, a professional photographer. To provide a modern perspective to his work, I had re-photographed all of Galbraith's original sites in 1996 and produced a series of "then and now" display boards. These panels also were shown in many of the same venues as the historical material and helped provide a fuller chronology for Yonge Street, right to the end of the bicentennial year.

The first regionally published edition was enthusiastically received and quickly sold. Now with the help of publisher Barry Penhale, a new trade edition is available to the growing number of individuals interested in Canadian and particularly Ontario history.

From the start, I participated in every aspect of this publication, provided many of the photographs, and even was involved in the distribution and sale of the first edition. However, this new book really is the culmination of the dedicated research by hundreds of historically minded individuals in Greater Toronto, York Region and Simcoe County. To all of them I dedicate this book.

RALPH MAGEL
NEWMARKET HISTORICAL SOCIETY

First Nations' Trail

In southern Ontario, the development of trails followed the use of watercourses and were determined by topography. Trails could not develop after the Ice Ages until the ice sheets had retreated far enough and the ground had become stable, with the routes of trails and the degree of their use influenced as well by the resolution of drainage into rivers and creeks of predictable courses.

Yonge, as an aboriginal trail, would not have formed until Lake Simcoe had formed and, at the time the first Europeans were entering the area, the lands to the south of Lake Simcoe were extremely swampy. South of the Oak Ridges Moraine, where Toronto's watercourses originate, there were many rivers to cross as well, and the trail, when formed, was less well-used than some others. Its aboriginal names are lost but the trail was used during the fur trade era by the Northwest Company and others.

Toronto Carrying Place Trail was a link in a chain of trails and water routes that extended from west and northern Canada to the Gulf of Mexico, widely used and mapped first after Contact — the name Toronto, attached to this trail is unclear in origin and date.

Davenport was the name given in the British Regime to what is Toronto's oldest road, formed at the end of the Ice Ages at the base of the escarpment across the city, which is the shoreline of the post Ice Age Lake Iroquois. The trail probably began as a route for animals which was adopted by Paleo-Indian peoples and used more extensively in succeeding eras. The trail linked the Humber with the Don River and connected with other, later, trails — its aboriginal names are not known.

Parliament was the trail along the top of the west bank of the Don River which led from the Davenport trail to the delta of the Don. At the foot of this trail, which was improved to serve as a very early road in the British Regime, were the first parliament buildings of Upper Canada, hence its present name.

Dundas was a trail that led westwards across the alluvial plain below the escarpment to link with the Toronto Carrying Place Trail and the Davenport Trail both east of the Humber. Together, both east-west trails were extended further west by Simcoe and his regiment and Dundas became known as "The Governor's Road".

Lakeshore was a trail of unknown date which appears only as fragments in early maps and records but which was well-used by Elizabeth Simcoe as she rode and walked through the region. It followed the shoreline of Lake Ontario and was influenced by rising and falling lake levels, inlets and rivers.

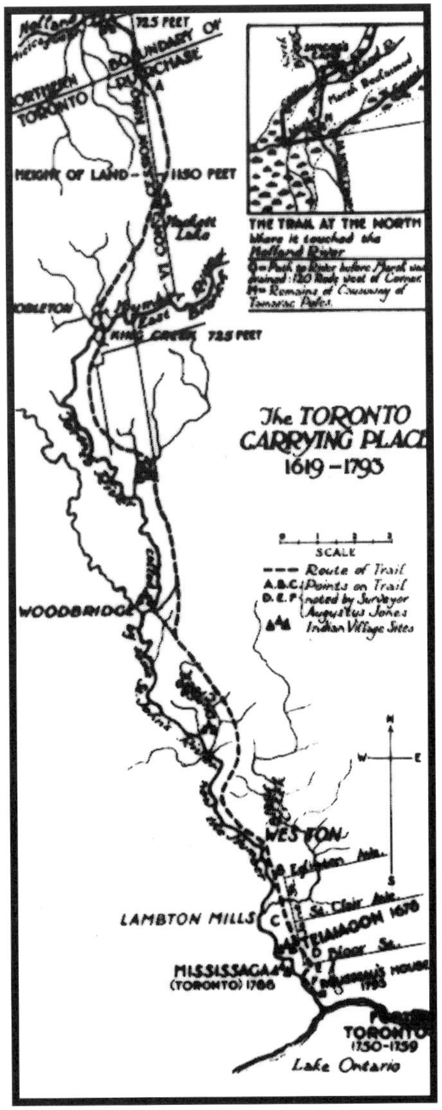
725 FEET
BOUNDARY OF PURCHASE
NORTHERN
TORONTO
HEIGHT OF LAND
1150 FEET
THE TRAIL AT THE NORTH
where it touched the
Holland River
KING CREEK 725 FEET
The TORONTO
CARRYING PLACE
1619–1793
SCALE
Route of Trail
A.B.C. D.E.F. Points on Trail noted by Surveyor Augustus Jones
Indian Village Sites
WOODBRIDGE
WESTON
LAMBTON MILLS
St. Clair Ave.
TEIAIAGON 1676
Bloor St.
MISSISSAGA
(TORONTO) 1788
TORONTO
1750-1759
Lake Ontario

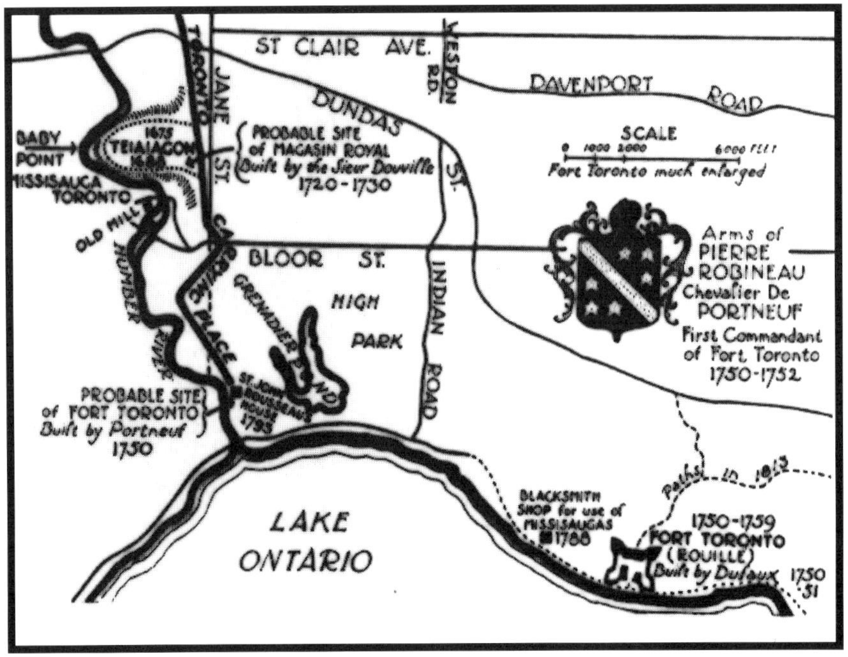
ST CLAIR AVE.
WESTON RD.
DAVENPORT ROAD
DUNDAS ST.
JANE ST.
BABY POINT
MISSISSAUGA TORONTO
1675 TEIAIAGON 1688
PROBABLE SITE of MAGASIN ROYAL Built by the Sieur Douville 1720-1730
SCALE
0 1000 2000 6000 FEET
Fort Toronto much enlarged
Arms of PIERRE ROBINEAU Chevalier De PORTNEUF
First Commandant of Fort Toronto 1750-1752
OLD MILL
BLOOR ST.
HUMBER RIVER
CARRYING PLACE
GRENADIER POND
HIGH PARK
INDIAN ROAD
PROBABLE SITE of FORT TORONTO Built by Portneuf 1750
LAKE ONTARIO
BLACKSMITH SHOP for use of MISSISSAUGAS 1788
1750-1759 FORT TORONTO (ROUILLE) Built by Dufaux 1750-51

FIRST NATIONS TRAILMAKERS

As the Ice Ages ended some 16,000 to 10,000 years ago, the first human beings entered the area. Although very little archaeology has been done in the Toronto region, the various periods of human habitation in southern Ontario have been classified by archaeologists:

• Paleo-Indian peoples living nomadic, hunting lives and using stone tools, from 10,000 to 7,000 B.C.

• Archaic peoples with worked stone and copper tools hunted throughout the region; the dugout canoe was developed in this period, from 7,000 to 1,000 B.C.

• Initial Woodland peoples developed the bow and arrow, clay vessels to replace those of skin and bark, and stone pipes for smoking tobacco, from 1,000 B.C. to 700 A.D.

• Ontario Iroquoians were linked by the same language roots and had agriculture and palisaded villages; they bore the contact with Europeans which dramatically altered their lives, from 700 to 1651 A.D. Wars with the Iroquois Confederacy to the south drove them away and they were replaced in southern Ontario by Algonkian peoples from the north: the branches of the great Ojibwa Nation which includes the Mississaugas.

• Historic peoples, from 1615 to 1900 A.D., underwent major cultural changes and relocations as the setting up of Reserves restricted their hunting and mobility; the Mississaugas buy back pieces of their own lands for Reserves and the Iroquois move into Canada permanently as United Empire Loyalists.

Painting is unidentified, but is probably Reverend Peter Jones (Kahkewaquonaby) January 1, 1802 - June 29, 1856

METRO/ONTARIO
THE GLOBE AND MAIL, THURSDAY, NOVEMBER 12, 1987 A21

Old Indian map has 'immense historical value,' expert says

BY MARK BOURRIE
Special to The Globe and Mail

A 350-year-old map with a mysterious past is giving historians, archeologists and geographers a unique glimpse of Eastern Canadian history.

The Taunton map, which was found in an archive in 1977, is the only surviving map that was drawn with an Indian concept of geography, John Steckley, an expert on native languages, says.

Mr. Steckley, a teacher at Toronto's Humber College, said the map was drawn with a distinctly Huron view of Ontario and parts of Quebec and New York State.

He said the map is the only surviving document showing the tribes that lived in Eastern Canada that were dispersed by the Iroquois in the 1640s.

The map details the Iroquois country south of Lake Ontario and the St. Lawrence River when the first white explorers, traders and priests arrived. It is also the first map to show all five of the Great Lakes, although the cartographer greatly underestimated the size of Lake Michigan, and the extent and shapes of the rest of the Upper Lakes were unclear to him.

The map was found by Conrad Heidenreich, a University of Toronto historical geographer, while researching documents for a section of the Historical Atlas of Canada. The document was unsigned and undated. A copy of the map is in the public archives in Ottawa, but the original remains in the Royal Navy archives in Taunton, England.

"As soon as I found it, I realized the significance of it," Mr. Heidenreich said. "First, it is the only known map that depicts the native groups of Eastern Canada prior to the Iroquois wars of the 1640s.

eventually ended up in the Royal Navy archives," Mr. Heidenreich said.

Mr. Steckley, an expert on the Huron language, said the map is of "immense historical value" because the names of places and Indian tribes were written in Huron, allowing historians to determine trade routes and native concepts of geography. The map was drawn on a piece of deer hide.

Mr. Heidenreich said debate now revolves around the question of who drew the map and when it was finished.

He said he believes the map was drawn in 1641, using information from three sources: a map by the explorer Samuel Champlain, which survives; a lost map by a Jesuit priest of the Huron view of their country and neighboring tribes, and a description of the Iroquois country from two French prisoners freed by the Iroquois in 1641.

He said scholars are still debating whether it was drawn by a surveyor or a Jesuit priest, who both lived at Quebec City in the 1640s.

Soon after the map was finished, the Iroquois confederacy struck at the native groups of Ontario, destroying the Huron, Petun, Neutral, Erie and Algonquin tribes and leaving Southern and Central Ontario almost empty for more than a century.

"It was a very bloody, very turbulent period of history. We are very fortunate to have this snapshot of what Ontario was like before the Iroquois holocaust," Mr. Heidenreich said.

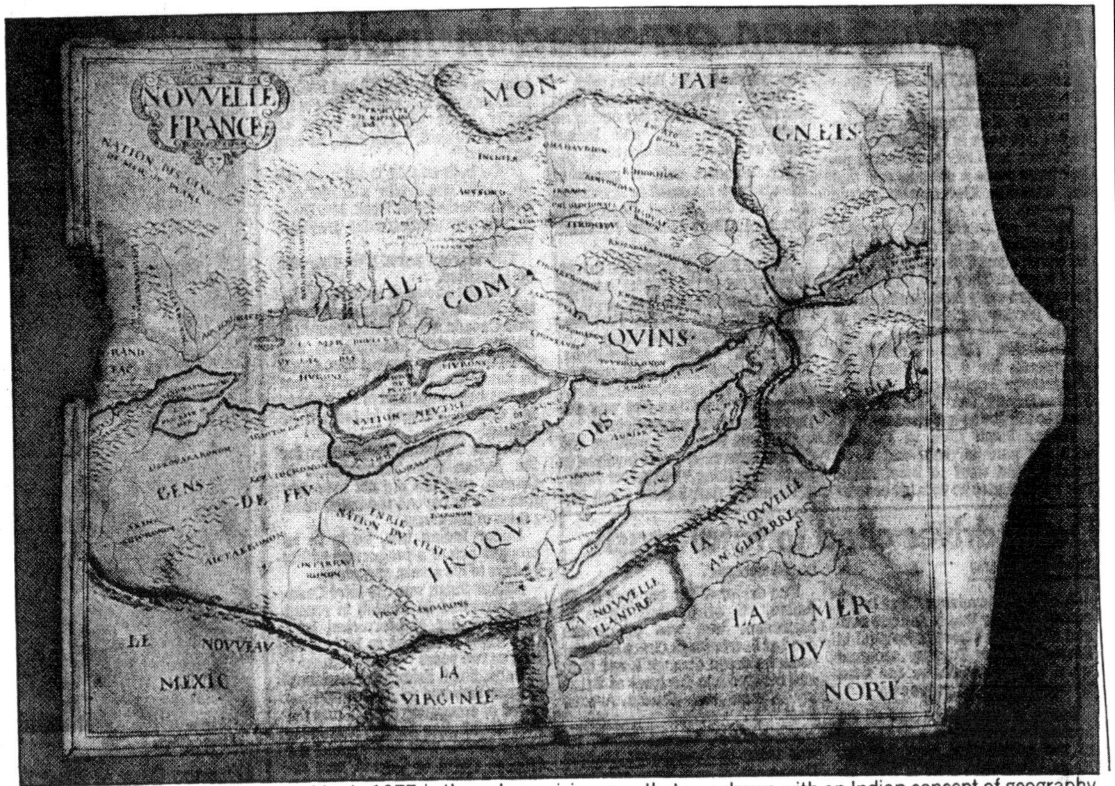

The Taunton map found in an archive in 1977 is the only surviving map that was drawn with an Indian concept of geography.

BUILDING OF YONGE STREET

TORONTO'S FOUNDER AND YONGE STREET

JEAN-BAPTISTE ROUSSEAUX

The first white man known to have chosen to live in the Toronto region and to build his home here, was Jean-Baptiste Rousseaux (1758-1812). As a trader like his father, Jean was conversant in several Indian languages, and French, English, and Latin. The trading license his father had been granted by the French Crown was inherited by Jean-Baptiste, and it was for the entire north shore of Lake Ontario. The common trading route along the Toronto Carrying Place Trail and the French forts gave the Rousseaux men a great deal of control.

Because of their extensive knowledge of the land and of the languages of indigenous peoples, the Rousseaux men served governments as official interpreters, a role that places Jean-Baptiste as the most important figure of his time. He was involved with the American Revolution and the coming of the Loyalists, the Constitution Act, land treaty negotiations with the Indians, and the development of Simcoe's Town of York.

Jean's first child had just been born when the Simcoe arrived, and it was he who gave the new governor shelter and food until their own quarters were established, having piloted their ship to safe harbour. All who had explored the Toronto Carrying Place Trail had known Rousseaux and been accommodated by him but Simcoe, who had great need of his skills and languages, for reasons not yet fully understood, did not like Rousseaux and refused to grant him the land where he had been living.

Rousseaux soon moved to Ancaster but kept his duties as an official interpreter. His home on the Humber was so well-known that surveyors used it as a base point for many years, with the British calling it "St. John's House" and the Humber "St. John's River". The upper of the maps to the right was done in 1792 by Joseph Bouchette for Simcoe, and the lower map was made in 1798. As the shift from French to British Regimes took place and the fur stocks were becoming exhausted, the Toronto Carrying Place Trail was still the primary route into and out of the area northwards, a role soon to be diminished with the building of mills. No picture is known to exist of Jean-Baptiste Rousseaux, although the precise location of his Humber home has been determined. Before he left for Ancaster, Yonge Street had been roughed out and was in use and the Toronto Carrying Place Trail interrupted by grants of lands to private individuals, through which it ran.

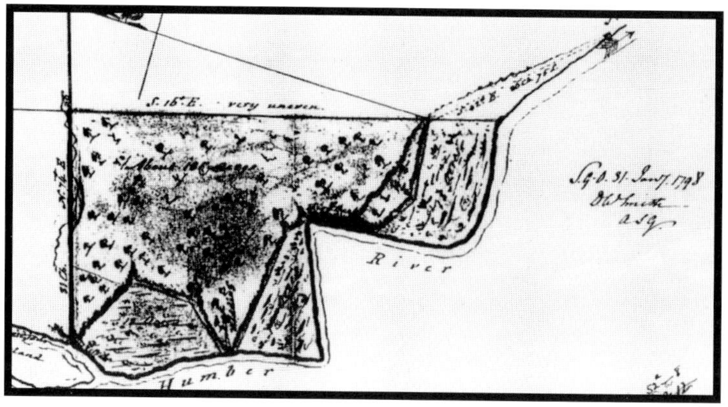

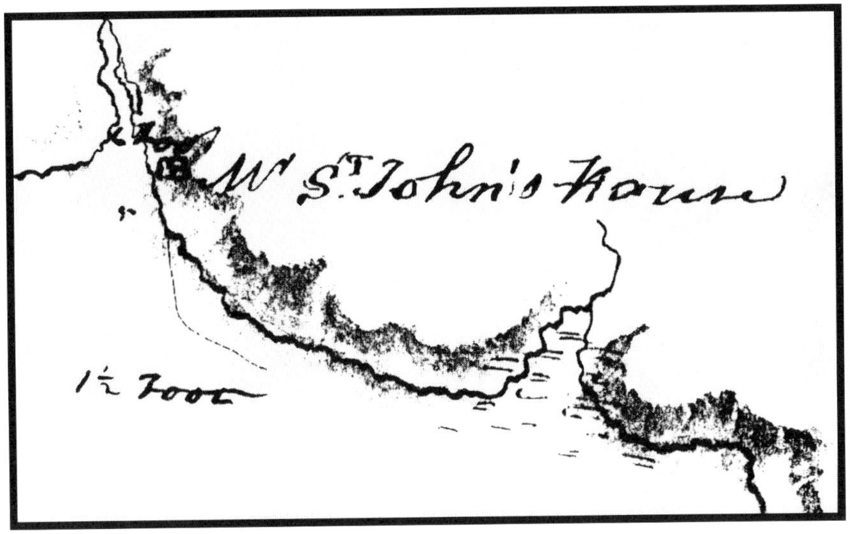
Wm St. John's House
1½ Foot

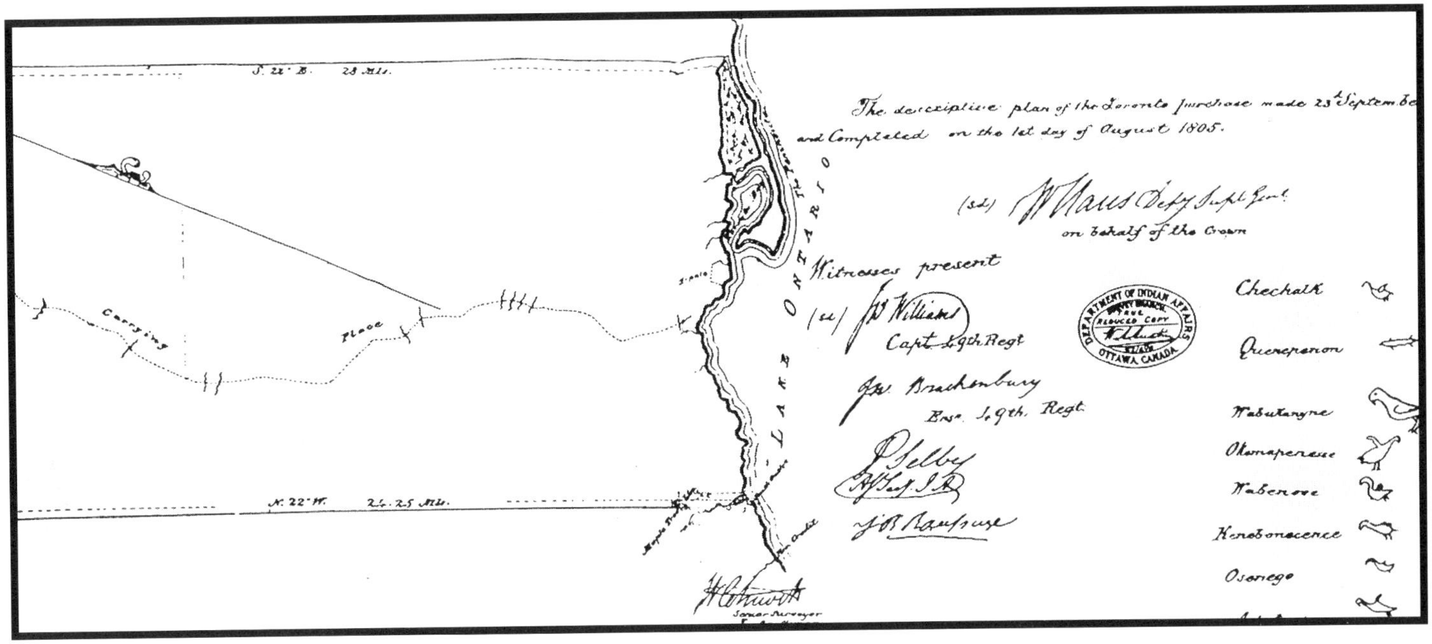
S. 22° E. 28 Mls.
N. 22° W. 26.25 Mls.
Carrying Place
LAKE ONTARIO
The descriptive plan of the Toronto purchase made 23d September
and Completed on the 1st day of August 1805.
(sd) on behalf of the Crown
Witnesses present
Capt. 49th Regt
Ens. 49th Regt
DEPARTMENT OF INDIAN AFFAIRS
TRUE REDUCED COPY
OTTAWA, CANADA
Chechalk
Quenepenon
Wabukanyne
Okemapenesse
Wabenose
Kenebonecence
Osenego

The French Regime

For two hundred years before the British took over the administration of the country, Canada was all French. From the time Jacques Cartier arrived, the French explored, recorded and mapped the new continent, penetrating into the far west and exploring south as far as the Gulf of Mexico. Each explorer built his knowledge upon that of his predecessors, and maps became increasingly more detailed and accurate. Heavily dependent upon the understanding and skill of the native peoples of North America, who had an intimate and comprehensive knowledge of the continent, the French formed good working relationships with most nations and were able to develop extensive trade. The explorers were missionaries, employees of the fur trading companies, independent traders and, later, surveyors and military engineers. Baron Armand-Louis de Lahontan (1666-1715) came to Canada in 1683 and, at age twenty-two, took charge of an expedition into the Great Lakes and west. While his map shown here is somewhat less accurate than that of his predecessors, it reveals much about French explorations up to that date, 1703. None other than the humorist Stephen Leacock admired Lahontan, not just for his exploration but also for the stories and other information published in his book "Nouveaux Voyages". Lahontan served briefly as the King's Lieutenant in Newfoundland, but ended his days in exile because of his rebellious nature and views. The first explorer to visit Upper Canada was the great Samuel de Champlain (1570-1635) who published his own map in 1616.

While explorations and recording continued, the trade in furs expanded dramatically during the French Regime. The usual route from the Montreal headquarters of the companies was up the Ottawa River, across the French-Severn system into the Upper Lakes, but as fur stocks became exhausted in the west, other routes were used. Chief among these in this region was the Toronto Carrying Place Trail which reached, as part of a system, from northern Canada to the Gulf of Mexico. The French built three forts in this area on the Toronto Carrying Place Trail.

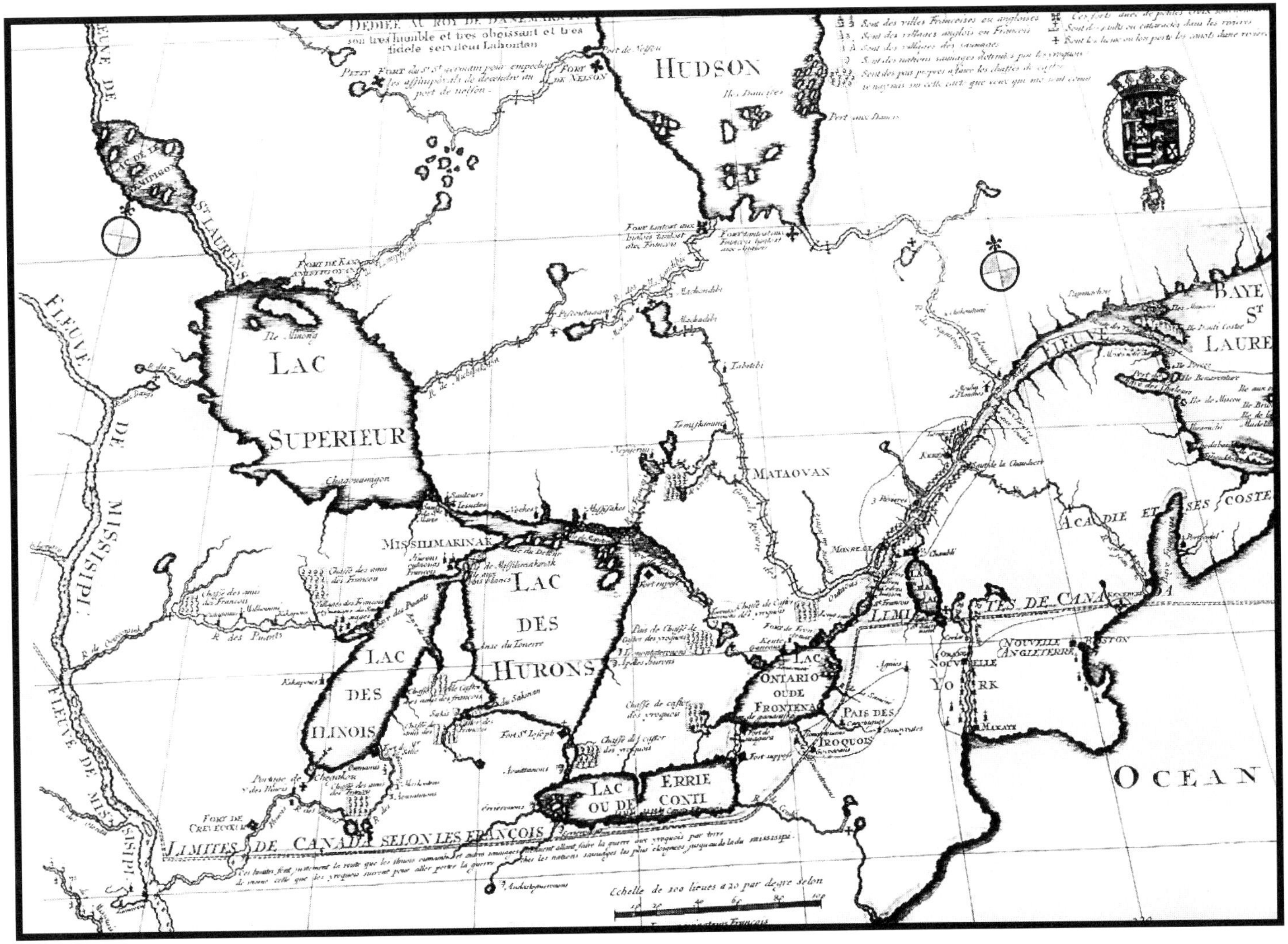
HUDSON
FORT DE NELSON
LAC SUPERIEUR
MISSILIMAKINAK
LAC DES HURONS
LAC DES ILINOIS
MATAOVAN
LAC ONTARIO OU DE FRONTENAC
LAC OU DE ERRIE CONTI
PAIS DES IROQUOIS
NOUVELLE YORK
NOUVELLE ANGLETERRE
BOSTON
ACADIE ET SES COSTES
FLEUVE DE MISSISIPI
LIMITES DE CANADA SELON LES FRANCOIS
OCEAN

The first of the forts was built at what is now the residential neighbourhood called Baby Point. This fort, Le Magasin Royale, was constructed in 1720 and had a village and boat yard attached to it. It was on the site of Teiaiagon, a Seneca Indian colony which itself was on the site of more ancient Indian communities. Trade quickly outgrew the fort and another, larger fort was built near the mouth of the Humber in 1740. The second structure was called Fort Toronto. Again, trade outgrew the facility and a third was built, Fort Rouillé, on the shoreline of Lake Ontario in 1750. Only the third fort has been excavated and studied, and its location, on the CNE grounds is marked by a monument. Like the others, Fort Rouillé had an attached community, a burial ground (later used by the British as well), and an Indian village existed to the north on the bank of Garrison Creek near today's Queen Street. Near the end of the fur trade era, the Northwest Company, which travelled the Don River-Davenport Trail to the trail that became Yonge Street had been hauling its boats, laden with trade goods, up the Yonge route with a winch and capstan. When Yonge Street was being built, the Northwest Company offered a large sum to assist with construction and improvements in the late 1790s.

The first European to see the Toronto region, Lake Ontario, Niagara Falls, and other locations, was Champlain's own assistant, Etienne Brulé (1592-1633) who had been in Canada since 1608. He was the first to learn to speak any Indian language and did so as a result of living with the Indians. With Champlain, he came to Huronia and, with only Huron warriors, then travelled south from Lake Simcoe down the Toronto Carrying Place Trail. He arrived at the mouth of the Humber River in 1615, and continued on to Niagara and points south. His discoveries, very numerous, are found in the accounts written by others.

Canise or Great Sail, the Chippewa chief, held Francis Simcoe in his arms at the naming of York. He was a great friend of John Graves Simcoe. This drawing of him (above) was rendered by Mrs. Simcoe. "He it was who told Simcoe of another route leading south from the East branch of the Holland River by which the swamps of the Carrying Place could be avoided." Excerpt from: The Yonge Street Story, by F. R. Bercham.

AUGUSTUS JONES, SURVEYOR

(circa 1757-16 November 1836)

Augustus Jones, a United Empire Loyalist from New York State, was instrumental in the surveying and clearing of Yonge Street.

Instructed by Lieutenant-Governor John Graves Simcoe to survey and clear what is now Yonge Street, Jones, accompanied by a party of Queen's Rangers, began the survey at Holland Landing, working his way south to York (Toronto). On February 20, 1796, he officially reported to Governor Simcoe that Yonge Street was open from York to Pine Fort Landing (Holland Landing) on Lake Simcoe.

Though there is some confusion about Augustus' personal life, it is known that he, his father, five brothers and one sister settled in Saltfleet Township on the Niagara Peninsula in 1789; his other sister, a widow, and her two teenaged children arrived the following year. Augustus apparently married twice and was the father of ten children. His first wife was Tuhbenahneequay, the daughter of Mississauga chief Wahbanosay. Their second son, Peter (Kahkewaquonaby), became a well-known Methodist minister and Chief of the Mississaugas of the Credit. Augustus's second wife was Sarah Tekahirogen, daughter of Henry Tekarhogen, a noted Mohawk warrior who was related to Joseph Brant by marriage. Augustus and Sarah's youngest son, Augustus, Jr., inherited his father's surveying instruments and also became a surveyor.

Augustus died on his farm at Cold Springs on November 16, 1836 and was buried on the banks of the Grand River. His body was later moved to Greenwood Cemetery in Brantford where it lies in an unmarked grave; his son Peter is buried in the same cemetery. More information about Augustus Jones and his family appears in the book *Researching Yonge Street*.

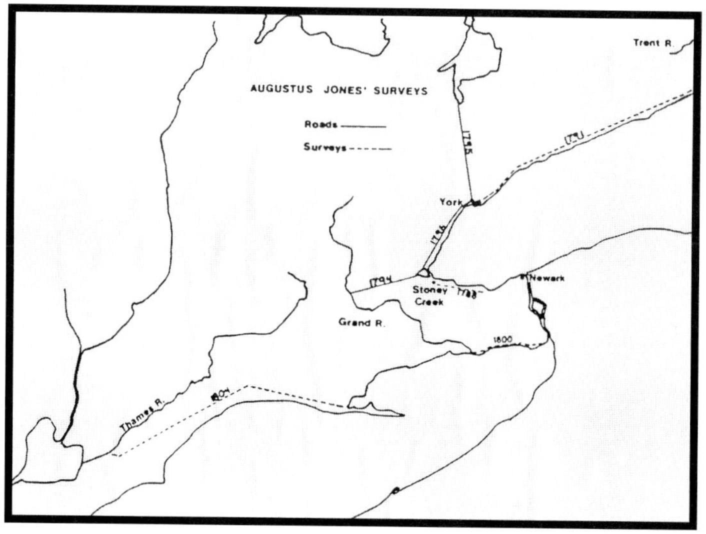

The above map is a record of the surveys done by Augustus Jones, including that of Yonge Street in 1794.

THE FAMILY OF AUGUSTUS JONES

Right, is a partial family tree. In some instances, sources consulted by the compiler give conflicting and/or contradictory information about the Jones family, particularly Augustus, his wives, and his children. Additional searching is required to determine the birth dates of Augustus and his siblings and, therefore, the birth order shown may not be accurate.

Augustus Jones (1757-1836)

AUGUSTUS JONES' SIBLINGS

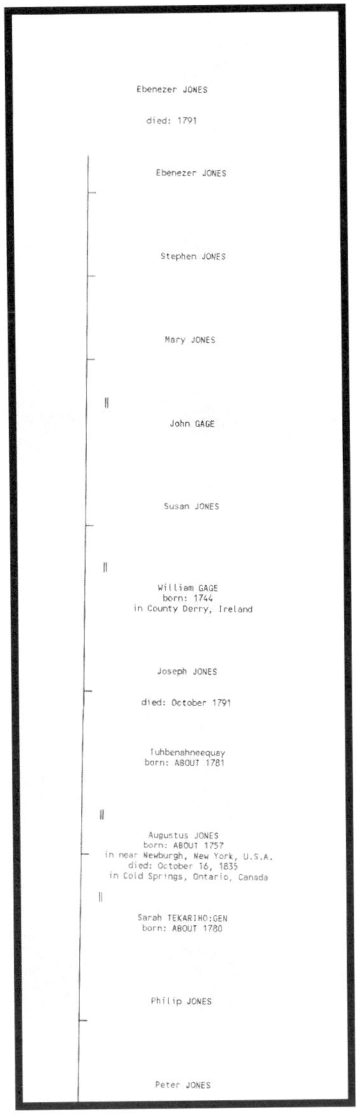

AUGUSTUS JONES' DESCENDANTS

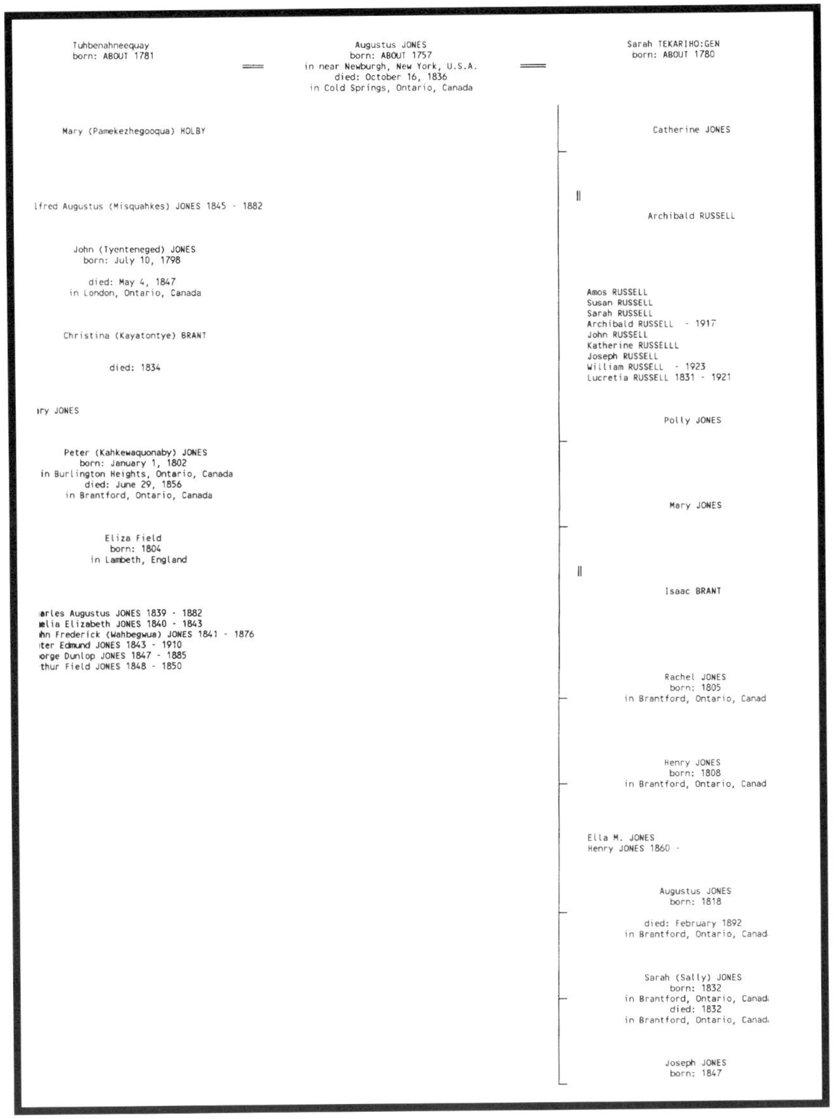

German Pioneers Build Yonge Street

Johann Ulrich Moll Berczy (1744-1813), known as William Moll Berczy, was a co-founder of Toronto, the founder of Markham, an artist, architect, pioneer, builder, developer of Yonge Street. He is remembered in Toronto's Berczy Park on Front Street, and on a plaque in Toronto's City Hall.

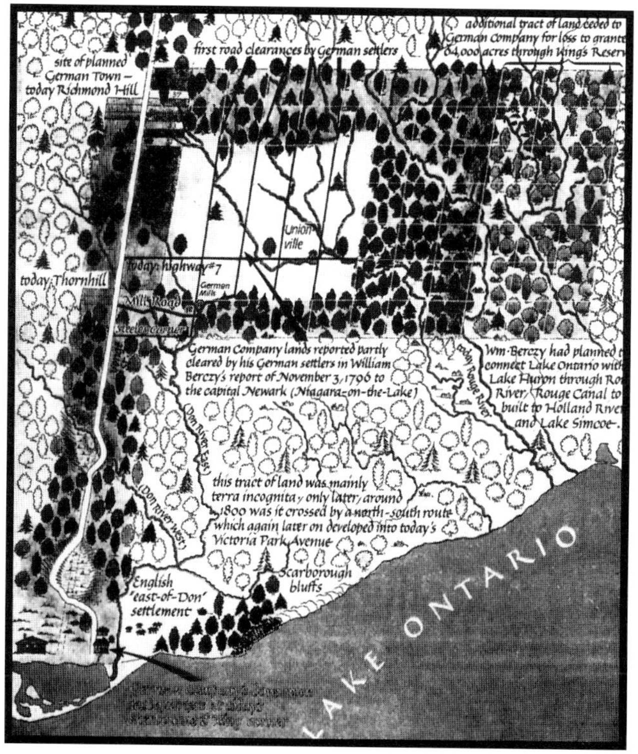

Illustration from a sketch by William Moll Berczy, preserved in the Public Archives of Canada.

Berczy settlers clearing virgin forest for Yonge Street are commemorated on the plaque at the cemetery on Old Kennedy Road in Unionville, and in the memorial in the Markham Town Centre.

EARLY SETTLERS

TOWNSHIP PAPERS

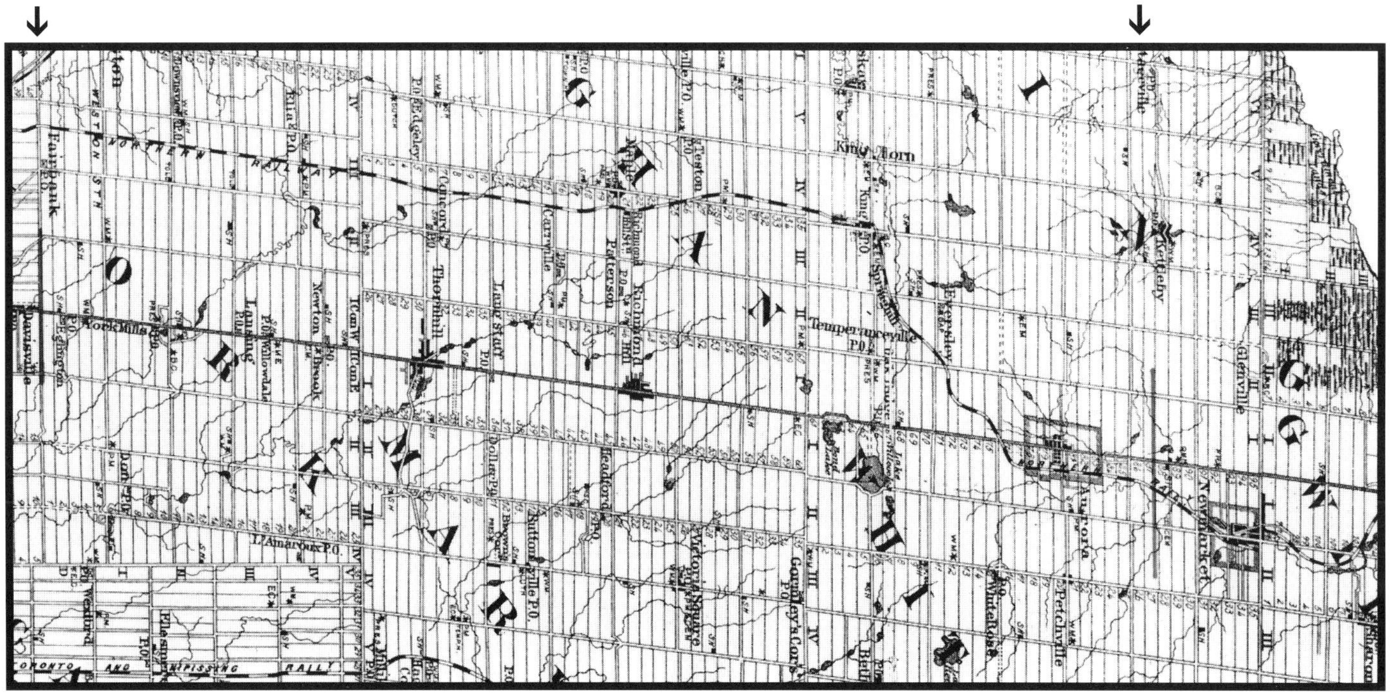

The section of map above is taken from Miles' 1878 Atlas and the area covered by the documents is between the arrows on this map.

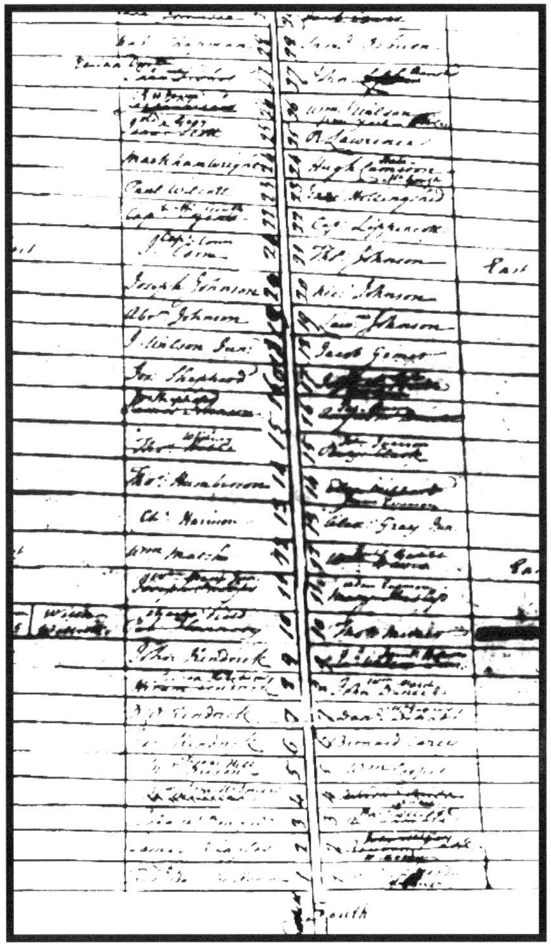
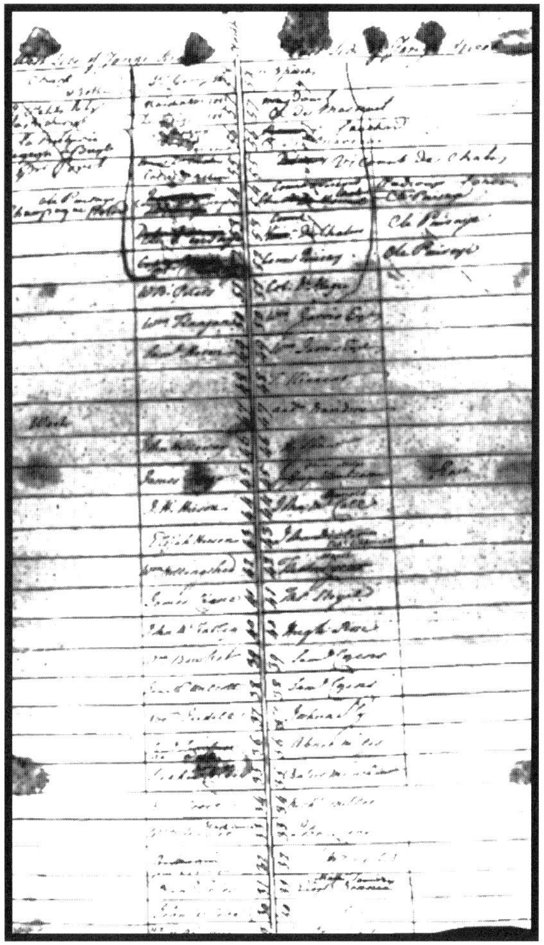
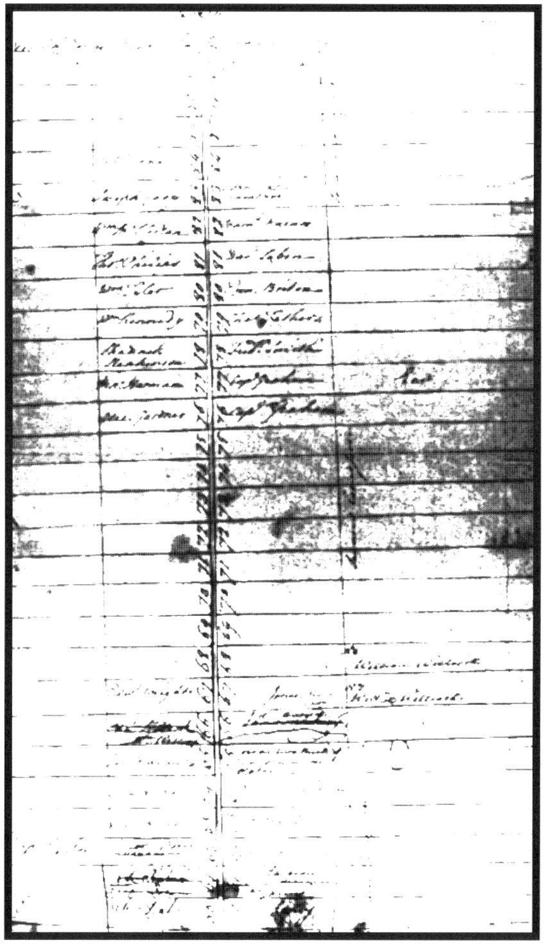

These three documents combine to provide a picture of landowners along Yonge Street (from Eglinton Avenue north to Aurora) in about 1798. They were found in a group of records at the Archives of Ontario, called "Township Papers". These early records are filed by township and then by concession and lot number. Although there is not a file for every lot, there are maps and other documents relating to the property and the settler, before a land patent was issued. These documents were filed with York Township.

ORIGINAL PATENTEES

Among the first people to settle and farm the lands along Yonge Street were the following, who received land grants, or patents, from the Crown. Among the requirements of land ownership, was the improvement and maintenance of the rough trail on which their properties fronted — Yonge Street.

1 JONATHAN SCOTT appears on the List of Inhabitants of York in 1797 as a single man and had his farm on Yonge Street on the southwest corner of Steeles Avenue.

2 MALCOLM WRIGHT appears on the same list in 1797 and his farm was on Yonge Street, just south of Jonathan Scott's.

3 PAUL WILLCUTT (WILCOTT) appears on the list in 1799 and was appointed an overseer of the highways on Yonge Street.

4 JOHN CONN was an ex-soldier living on Yonge Street who received a lot on the southwest corner of George and Duchess Streets.

5 JOSEPH JOHNSON was a member of the family who held extensive holdings on Yonge Street between Finch and Steeles Avenues. He was elected a Constable of York in 1797. Other members of the family were Abraham, James, Lawrence, Nicholas, Thomas and William Johnson.

6 JOSEPH SHEPARD (d 1837) was an Indian trader and radical Reformer who settled on Yonge Street at Sheppard Avenue, which was named after him. The Shepard family owned one of the largest and most productive brickworks in Yorkville. The family name has been variously spelled Shepard, Sheperd, Sheppard and Shepherd.

7 THOMAS HILL was a sergeant in the Queen's Rangers who served throughout the American Revolution. He kept a tavern on Yonge Street at Lansing and appears on the List of Inhabitants of York in 1797.

8 THOMAS HUMBERSTONE was appointed a pathmaster on Yonge Street in 1812. He does not appear in the List of Inhabitants of York before that date.

9 CHRISTOPHER HARRISON first appears on the list in 1800.

10 WILLIAM MARSH JR. first appears on the list in 1802.

11 JOSEPH PHELPS appears on the list in 1797.

12 KENDRICK BROTHERS There were four brothers with adjoining lots on the west side of Yonge Street north of Lawrence Avenue.

DUKE WILLIAM KENDRICK (b 1766?-1813) Not much is known about him, but it is known that he played an active role in the early governance of York, being elected a constable for the Town in 1797. He died on January 1, 1813 while on active duty as lieutenant of the 3rd Regiment of York Militia;

JOHN KENDRICK (b 1764?) was High Constable of York from 1800 to 1803;

JOSEPH KENDRICK was master of several vessels on the Lake and served during the War of 1812 on the Prince Regent;

HIRAM KENDRICK also had a town lot on the west side of George Street.

The **Kendricks** worked as house-builders, but were mainly interested and employed on the lakes as sailors.

13 JOHN MCDOUGALL was a Highland Scotsman who served in the British Commissariat as a conductor of wagons in the American Revolution. After the war, he moved to Shelburne, N.S., where he kept a store. He later came to Upper Canada and kept a tavern in York for many years. About 1803, he moved to his lot on Yonge Street north of Eglinton Avenue and kept a tavern there. He was the grandfather of the Hon. William McDougall.

14 JAMES RUGGLES (d 1804) With his younger brother Nathaniel, he was the nephew of Brigadier General Timothy Ruggles, who served in the army under Lord Amherst and was one of the most prominent Massachusetts Loyalists. They belonged to the sixth generation of their family in Massachusetts, and kept a shop on Yonge Street. James Ruggles was made an Ensign in the York Militia in 1798 and was later drowned in the loss of the Speedy. Nathaniel declined to serve in the Militia.

15 SIR DAVID WILLIAM SMITH (SMYTH) (1764-1837) The son of Lieutenant Colonel John Smith came to Canada from England in 1790 and was elected a member of the Legislative Assembly in 1792, 1796 and 1800; speaker in 1797-9 and 1801-4; appointed to the Executive Council in 1796 and was made surveyor-general in 1800. He returned to England in 1804 but continued to receive a pension - a emolument that was one of William Lyon Mackenzie's chief subjects of complaint. Smith wrote a topographical survey of the province in 1799 and was created a baronet in 1821.

16 JOHN ELMSLEY SR. (1762-1805) Called to the English bar in 1796, he was appointed chief justice of Upper Canada in 1796 and was transferred to the same office in Lower Canada in 1802. During the first years of Lieutenant Governor Peter Hunter's administration, he was probably the most influential man in Upper Canada. His son, John Jr., was a member of the Executive Council (1831-3 and 1836-8) and of the Legislative Council (1831-41).

17 DR. JAMES MACAULEY (1759-1822) Born in Scotland, he was an army surgeon in the 33rd Regiment, and resigned the surgeoncy of the Botany Bay Corps to come to Upper Canada with John Graves Simcoe. He was appointed Deputy-Inspector General of Hospitals. In 1819 he was made the first president of the newly-formed Medical Board of Upper Canada, a position he held until his death. His was the first park-lot northwest of Queen and Yonge which later developed into the first suburb of Toronto and was called Macauleytown.

18 RICHARD LAWRENCE appears on the List of Inhabitants of York in 1797.

19 HUGH CAMERON first appears on the list in 1799.

20 ISAAC HOLLINGSHEAD is mentioned in Ely Playter's Diary and on the List of Inhabitants of York in 1797.

21 JOHN MCBRIDE There were two John McBrides in York at this time. The one who lived on Yonge Street was a Loyalist and may have become the doorkeeper to the Executive and Legislative Councils. He died in 1801.

22 PATRICK BERN (BURNS) settled in York Township on the east side of the Don River and raised a large family. Appears on the List of Inhabitants of York in 1797.

23 STILLWELL WILLSON both Sr. and Jr. first appear on the List of Inhabitants of York in 1808.

24 ELSA MILLARD does not appear on any List of Inhabitants of York.

25 ALEXANDER GRAY JR. first appears on the list in 1800, as does Alexander Gray Sr.

26 WILLIAM DAVIS does not appear on any List of Inhabitants of York.

27 J.C. THOMAS COCHRANE (1777-1804) Appointed puisne judge of the court of the King's Bench in 1803, he was drowned in the wreck of the Speedy a year later.

28 JOHN WILSON (b 1740?) Was a lessee of the King's Mill on the Humber and appointed a Captain in the York Militia in 1798.

28 JOHN WILSON JR. mentioned in Ely Playter's Diary and may be the son of the above John.

29 DANIEL DEHART SR. was elected an overseer of the highways for Yonge Street and appears on the List of Inhabitants of York in 1797 along with his son, Daniel DeHart Jr.

30 BERNARD CAREY was a Loyalist recommended by the Duke of Portland and appears on the list in 1797.

31 WILLIAM COOPER (1761?-1840) He was born in Bath, England, and settled in York in 1793, and, in a petition dated 1823, claimed to have built the first house there. He taught school, read prayers on Sundays, was an auctioneer, and owned various enterprises including a tavern, the Toronto Coffee House. In 1806 he built a grist and sawmill on the Humber River, and he also owned a wharf at the foot of Church Street which he sold in 1830.

32 WILLIAM WEEKES (d 1806) An Irishman who studies law in the United States, he came to York in 17098 and was elected to the Legislative Assembly in 1805. He was killed in a duel with William Dickson.

33 RICHARD GAMBLE Granted the lot on the east side of Yonge Street, between Eglinton and Lawrence Avenues, he disappears from the List of Inhabitants of York after 1799. His brother Nathaniel Gamble had Yonge Street lots too and, for a time, kept a tavern Nathaniel Jr. served in the list Regiment of York Militia during the War of 1812.

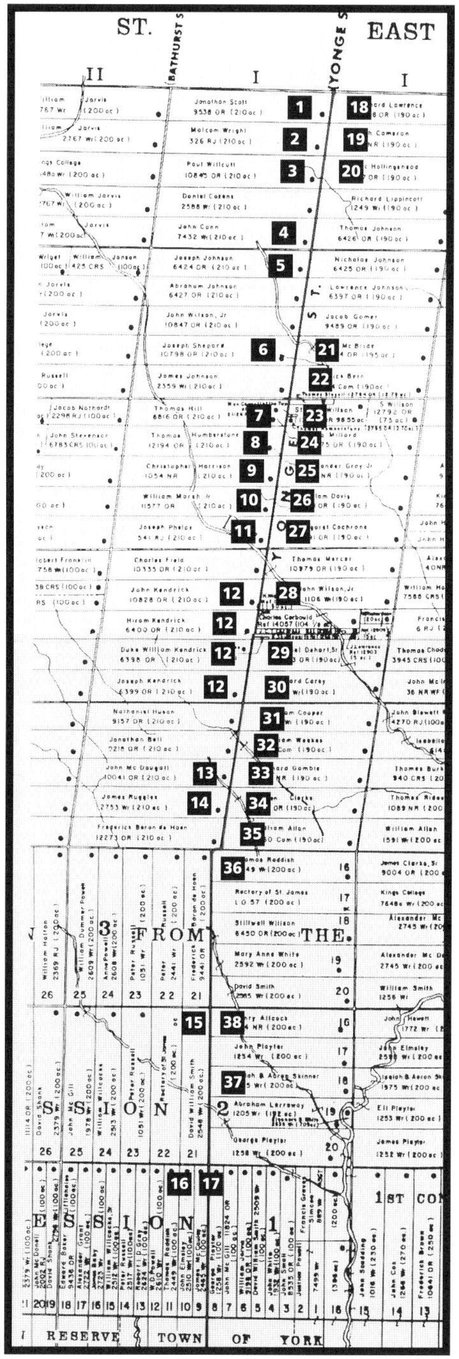

34 REUBEN CLERKE does not appear on any List of Inhabitants of York, either as Clark(e) or Clerke.

35 WILLIAM ALLAN (1770-1853) Born near Huntly, Aberdeenshire, he came first to Montreal in 1787 and worked as a junior clerk with Forsyth, Richardson & Co. Sometime prior to the spring of 1796, he came to York where he opened a general store and built a wharf. From 1797 to 1801, he was in partnership with Alexander Wood and was also appointed Collector of Customs, Inspector of Stills and Taverns, Postmaster of York, and Treasurer of the Home District. In 1798, he was appointed a Lieutenant in the York Militia, and later became a Major. As a Colonel in the 3rd Regiment, he was active during the War of 1812. The financial genius of the Family Compact and probably the wealthiest man in Upper Canada, he became the first president of the Bank of Upper Canada, a commissioner of the Canada Company, and a member of the Legislative Council (1825-41) and the Executive Council (1836-41), among the many posts he held.

36 REV THOMAS RADDISH (Reddish) The first clergyman in York, he arrived in 1796 to shepherd the Anglican congregation but left Canada six months later. As the Bishop of Quebec, Jacob Mountain, observed, "after a little speculation in land he [Raddish] returned to England, and we have heard no more of him."

37 ISAIAH & AARON SKINNER They were the sons of Timothy Skinner, a Loyalist from New Jersey, who came to Niagara in 1784 and built a mill there. By 1796, Isaiah and Aaron built a grist mill on the east bank of the Don River, a mile above Castle Frank and both played a role in the early governance of York; Isaiah was an overseer of the roads in his area.

38 HENRY ALLCOCK (d 1808) An English lawyer called to the bar in 1791, who became a judge of the court of the King's Bench of Upper Canada in 1798, succeeded John Elmsley as Chief Justice in 1802. After becoming Speaker of the Legislative Council in Upper Canada in 1803, he once again succeeded Elmsley and became Chief Justice of Lower Canada in 1805.

Among those rewarded with Yonge Street grants were some of the prominent United Empire Loyalists of the time. These military leaders included Capt. Richard Lippincott, Capt. George Playter, Baron Frederick de Hoen and Capt. Daniel Cozens Sr. For an account of their lives, please see the following pages.

The First Loyalists on Yonge Street

WHO WERE THE LOYALISTS?

Loyalists were those Americans who:

- resided in what is now the continental United States before the Revolutionary War of 1775-1783
- remained loyal to George III during the Revolution
- took up arms as soldiers in one of the American loyalist provincial corps
- had property and/or possessions confiscated because of loyalty to the Crown
- settled in British North America after the Revolution

Contrary to popular myth, a large percentage of Loyalists were of non-British extraction. Many were of German, Swiss, French, Dutch, American Indian and African descent. Loyalists transcended all social classes from wealthy merchants to farmers and tradespeople.

AMERICAN LOYALIST PROVINCIAL CORPS

Loyal colonists joined the Royal Standard in Regiments such as the King's Royal Regiment of New York, Butler's Rangers, the Loyal American Regiment, the New Jersey Volunteers, and Delancy's Brigade. Of the more than forty Loyalist battalions of the Provincial Corps "none earned greater distinction than the Queen's Rangers" said Stewart Bull in "The Queen's York Rangers".

QUEEN'S RANGERS IN THE AMERICAN REVOLUTION

Originally Roger's Rangers in the Seven Years War, the Queen's Rangers (King's Rangers at first) were raised in 1776 under Robert Rogers. John Graves Simcoe commanded the regiment as of 15 October 1777. It served with distinction throughout the conflict, in the Pennsylvania Campaign at Brandywine, Germantown and Monmouth, in the New Jersey-New York campaign at Long Island and Staten Island, at Kingsbridge, and in the Virginia campaign at Williamsburg. It was given at least two honours in that it was called the First American Regiment and honourably enrolled in the regular British Army.

QUEEN'S RANGERS OF UPPER CANADA, 1791-1802

Lieutenant Colonel John Graves Simcoe proposed that a Corps of troops be raised that would serve the dual role of military and civil service. They would work in the construction of various public works projects such as buildings, roads and bridges, as well as being available for military duties should the need arise. Secretary of War. Sir George Yonge, informed Simcoe that the Corps would wear the green uniforms of the same pattern as that worn by the late Corps of Queen's Rangers of the Revolutionary War. Simcoe had kept in contact with officers of this old regiment who had settled in the St. John River valley, such as Captain Aeneas Shaw and Captain John McGill, and those who had returned to England such as Captain David Shank, Captain Samuel Smith and Lieutenant William Jarvis. These gentlemen eagerly took up Simcoe's call for service in the new regiment. Thus, the Loyalist link!

YONGE STREET

In late 1795, Deputy Provincial Surveyor Augustus Jones, perhaps a Loyalist himself, was directed by Simcoe, now Lieutenant-Governor of Upper Canada, to survey and open a road based on an Indian trail that Simcoe himself had walked. Jones began his work immediately. The Rangers began at Lot 1 East and West of Yonge at Eglinton Avenue and worked up to Lot 17, just north of today's Sheppard Avenue. By August, the surveyor and Rangers had reached Lot 29, just south of Thornhill. The Rangers were then reassigned to military duties in the west, probably at Detroit, and the work of continuing the survey and building the road was done by the Berczy settlers.

"N.B. Those Loyalists who have adhered to the Unity of the Empire and joined the Royal Standard before the Treaty of Separation in the year 1783, and all their Children and their Descendants by either sex, are to be distinguished by the following Capitals affixed to their names U.E. alluding to their great principle, The Unity of the Empire"

The Queen's York Rangers working on Yonge Street in 1795

(courtesy of C.W. Jefferys Collection, Public Archives of Canada)

THE FIRST LOYALISTS ON YONGE STREET

1 **Captain Richard Lippincott** was born in New Jersey in 1745 and married Esther Bron in 1775. He served during the Revolution as a Captain. In 1782 he became involved in a controversy when he hanged Captain Joshua Huddy, a rebel prisoner in his charge, in retaliation for the killing of a Loyalist named Philip White for whom Huddy was to be exchanged. General George Washington made several attempts to have General Sir Henry Clinton, his counterpart in the British forces, surrender Captain Lippincott for this incident. It resulted in several small diplomatic incidents between British, French and Americans. Lippincott went first to New Brunswick, then lived for a year in England before settling in Vaughan Township in 1793. He received a total of 3000 acres of land granted in York, much of it in close proximity to Yonge, and was later granted more land in Richmond Hill. There, Richard Vanderburgh, son of a Loyalist, built his home which stands today as the office of the Richmond Hill Chamber of Commerce. Captain Lippincott died at Toronto in 1826. His only child, Esther Bordon, married Colonel George Taylor Dennison.

Captain James Fulton was a resident of New Hampshire where, in 1778, he was banished and had his property seized because of his loyalty. In 1782, he was serving as a Captain in the King's American Dragoons. He moved first to New Brunswick, then to Markham Township where he acquired land fronting on Yonge Street in Richmond Hill from Richard Lippincott. The land went to his daughter, Elizabeth, who had married Richard Vanderburgh, mention above, and it was their matrimonial home which is used by the Chamber of Commerce at Church and Weldrick Streets. Fulton eventually moved to Nova Scotia where he served as a magistrate. He died in 1826 in Halifax.

2 **Daniel Cozens** was a Captain with the New Jersey Volunteers. With his sons, he settled on this Lot in York County.

3 **Frederick Baron de Hoen** was almost a Loyalist. Although he took up arms in the American Revolution and although he settled in British North American after the War, he had been a professional soldier, a German Hessian, and had not resided in what is now the continental United States. Despite this, he was given a generous amount of land and served as a Captain in the York Militia. He farmed Lot 1 at the northwest corner of Yonge and Eglinton. He had financial difficulties and died unmarried around 1816.

4 **Colonel George Playter** was the founder of the Playter family of Toronto and North York. He was born at Wapping-on-the-Thames River in Surrey, and emigrated to New Jersey where he met Elizabeth Welding, a Quaker, and married her in 1765. He owned considerable property in the Philadelphia area which was confiscated as a result of his Loyalist sympathies. He served as an office in the British army during the Revolution and was forced to move to Canada with other Loyalists. Initially, he was at Kingston, then moved to York where he received numerous land grants on or near Yonge Street, most notably Park Lot 8 along the east side of Yonge from Queen to Bloor. Other lots he was granted were on Yonge between Thornhill and Richmond Hill. He resided near Castle Frank where he died about 1832.

John Dennis owned a respectable one-storey white wooden cottage on the northeast corner of Yonge and King Streets. Earlier, he had been superintendent of the Kingston dockyards. As a Loyalist, he received lands on the Humber River near the Village of Weston. The Dennis family is notable for their fine shipbuilding and contributions to maritime history.

5 **Captain John McGill** was born in Scotland and moved to Virginia before the Revolution. After the outbreak of hostilities he joined the Queen's Rangers (1st American Regiment) where he was a Captain and Commander of an infantry company of the regiment during the

Revolution. The company was involved in the Virginia Campaign of 1781. After the Revolution, McGill went to New Brunswick where he received two land grants, one in Parrtown and the other in Kingston Parish in King's County. In 1792, he responded to the request of John Graves Simcoe and joined the Queen's Rangers being raised for service in Upper Canada. In March 1792, he set out with Aeneas Shaw and David Shank, and snowshoed from New Brunswick to join Simcoe in York, Upper Canada. He was Adjutant of the new regiment and probably held that rank during the building of Yonge Street. He became a member of the Legislative Assembly and held his position until his death in 1834. He was granted a number of Lots in the vicinity of Yonge Street, and lived at "McGill's Cottage" on the site of the present Metropolitan United Church. McGill Street is named for him.

6 **William Jarvis** was an officer in the Queen's Rangers and was wounded in the siege of Yorktown. When the Queen's Rangers were reorganized as a military/civil corps by Simcoe, Jarvis was given a political appointment as Secretary of the Province. Jarvis Street was named for his son, Samuel Peters Jarvis. The family is notable for having given Toronto a number of sheriffs.

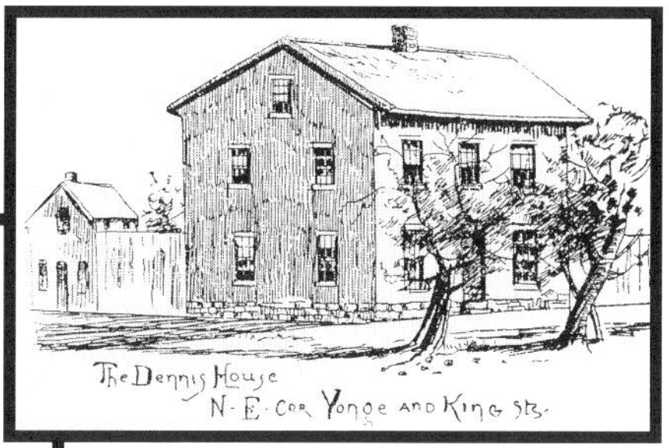

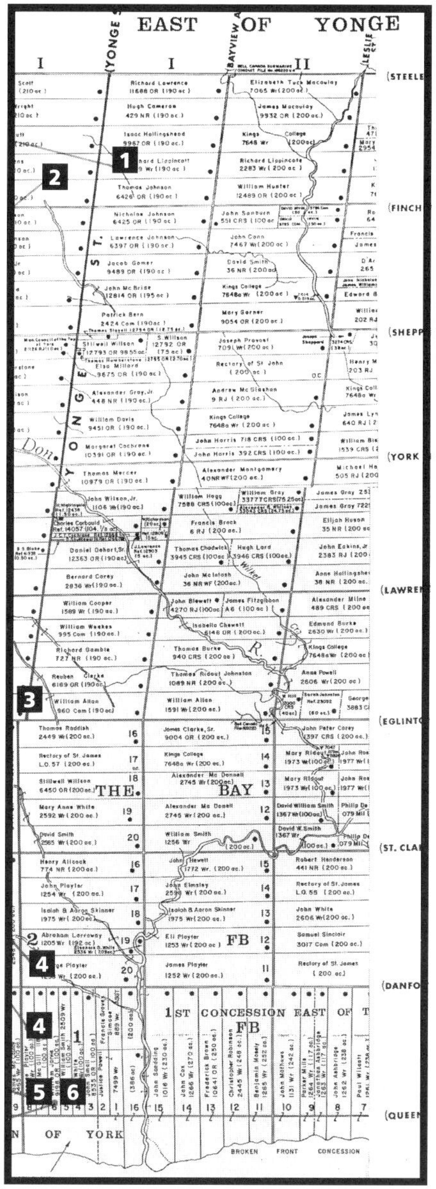

YONGE BUILDINGS AT BLACK CREEK

THE FLYNN HOUSE

This building stood on the southwest corner of Yonge Street just south of Drewry on Lot 22 of the First Concession West of Yonge in Newtonbrook. Daniel Flynn bought two village lots on 31 May 1858 and built this home for his family. Later, it was the home of his daughter, "Miss Flynn".

THE FLYNN BOOT AND SHOE SHOP

The shop was just south of the Flynn house on Yonge Street in Newtonbrook village. Between 1858 and 1885, Daniel worked here. It was then sold to his daughter, Jane Brennan, whose husband was also a shoemaker. Built of the same materials, it was probably constructed at the same time as the house.

RICHMOND HILL MANSE

Located on the east side of Yonge north of Major Mackenzie Drive, the house was built around 1835. In the 1840's, the local Presbyterians purchased it for the Rev. William Jenkins who is credited with introducing Presbyterianism to western Ontario. The building is in the Loyalist neo-classical style. Its unusual construction method, "plank-on-plank", consisted of 2 x 6 planks nailed on top of the others. A fund-raising drive was instituted to move the house to Black Creek Pioneer Village, and the sign for this campaign shows in the Yonge Street picture. The sign explains that the house moves along at 10¢ per foot; as the fund increased, the sign moved along Yonge Street from Major Mackenzie to Steeles. When the house was moved for real, it arrived at Black Creek Pioneer Village in 1978.

THE ROWLAND BURR LINK

Another Black Creek Pioneer Village link to Yonge is the fact that Rowland Burr, an engineer, was contracted in 1833 to improve Yonge Street. He graded the hills, straightened the road at York Mills, partially filled the bog and drained the swamp at the foot of the hill near the mills.

WHY WE NEED ROADS

AUGUSTUS JONES' YONGE STREET

This is Augustus Jones' drawing of his survey of the route for Lieutenant-Governor Simcoe's new road. The map, in the Archives of Ontario, is in colour and is dated 1794. Notice that Jones began his count from what is now Bloor Street, and marked out each mile thereafter. He has indicated the major river crossings and sections of the original Indian trail.

Jones' directions were to survey a road and "communications" from York (Toronto) to Nottawasaga Bay. At Mile 31, or Gwillimbury, travellers were expected to make their way by water up Lake Simcoe, past fields of corn cultivated by the Indians amidst oak forests, past an old trading post, to connect with another Old Indian trail leading northwest to Matchedash River. His assessment of the conditions for road development in this section are clear.

When the Berczy settlers went to work, they laid the road in as far as Gwillimbury.

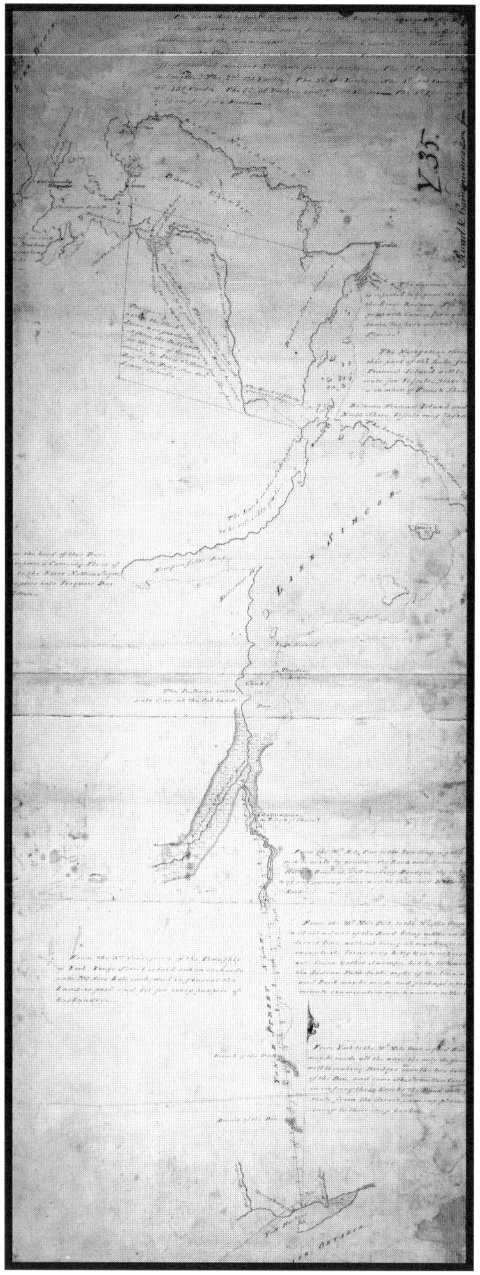

Upper Canada Roads in 1796

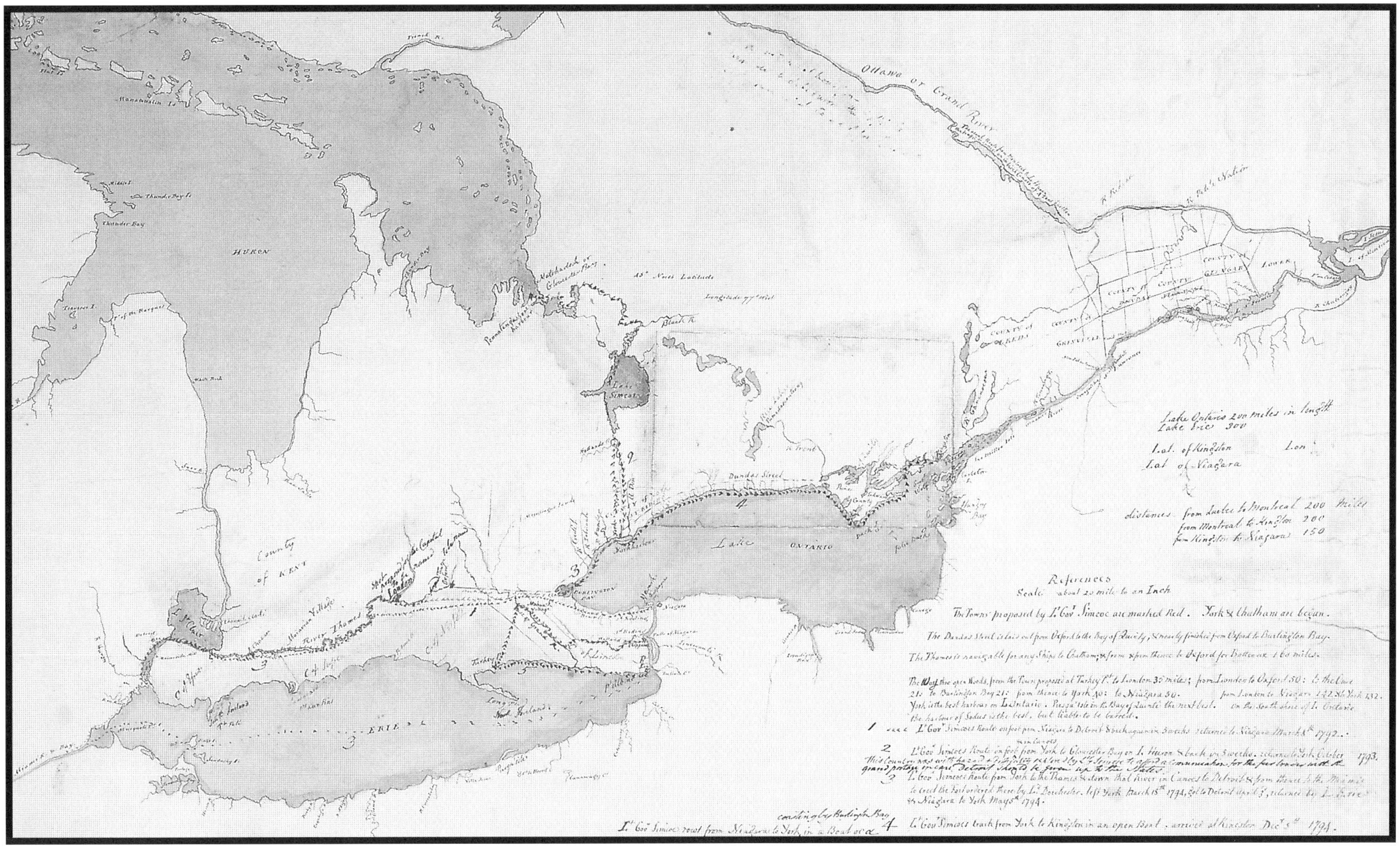

The Governor's Road

Lieutenant-Governor John Graves Simcoe, commissioned the building of Yonge and Dundas Street and Kingston Road.
(Courtesy of Metropolitan Toronto Public Library)

The term "The Governor's Road" was first coined in the 1790s to refer to the proposed road, Dundas Street, to connect Niagara with York. Lieutenant-Governor John Graves Simcoe was anxious to establish a military link between the Lakes of Ontario, Erie, St Clair and Huron and, in 1793, his own Queen's Rangers regiment began construction. The route was to serve as a military portage road. He insisted it be far enough north of Lake Ontario to be out of range of American attacks from the water. At first, Simcoe ordered Surveyor Alexander Aitken to begin making the road in 1794, but Aitken was already busy constructing Yonge Street and, therefore, did not get very far on the Governor's Road. Nonetheless, Aitken was able to open Dundas Street between York and Burlington that same year. At this point, construction began to slow down as Aitken turned his attention to Yonge Street once more.

Annoyed at the delay, acting Surveyor General, D.W. Smith, commissioned Augustus Jones, Deputy-Surveyor, to complete the road in July of 1795. When it was completed, the Governor's Road became the spinal cord which supported the settlement of Southern Ontario. The second oldest road in Ontario was named for the then Secretary of State in the British Government, Henry Dundas.

As it passed through the Mississauga Tract, which later became Toronto Township and part of Mississauga, Dundas Street promoted the establishment of such villages as Summerville, Dixie, Cooksville and Springfield (later Erindale), and the development of the surrounding area.

Transportation

For the first two hundred years or more, travellers in the region were dependent upon their own strength, in walking, snowshoeing, and paddling a canoe laden with their necessities. Most of these skills and the equipment were obtained from the Indians, who also taught the use of dog teams and sleds. As soon as it became possible, oxen and horses were brought in to undertake heavy work, but animals had to be fed and housed during the winters. Some found it useful to share their quarters with the animals until enough time and energy could be found to construct separate sheds. The first years were the hardest, and depended upon human strength almost entirely.

Within York/Toronto, public transportation began with H. B. Williams' Omnibus service, which ran from Yorkville's Town Hall to St Lawrence Market. In 1858, Williams was driven out of business by an entrepreneur with good political connections who established the first street railway on exactly the same route. A cabinetmaker and undertaker, Williams had built his own vehicles. This picture is all that survives of Williams' effort. The street railway kept as many as 1500 horses in the stable on Yorkville Avenue.

Deep snows and bitter winters were normal in the 19th and early 20th centuries, and created major problems for urban transportation systems. The street railway had tried various methods for clearing its routes and, in 1891, introduced a snowplow pulled by twelve dapple-grays. The public flocked to see the big team in action.

Above Inset: This 1907 view shows several modes of transportation: a variety of wagons and carts for hauling freight, horse-drawn omnibuses, a covered cab driven by a man in a top hat and, in the background, the upper decks and smokestack of a waiting steamboat. The ease in changing from one system to another would soon disappear.

Well into this century, much travel was done by water in various types of craft propelled by people themselves – in sailing boats and steamboats. On land, as roads developed, intercity stagecoach routes developed. George Player was among the first to develop a system and sold it shortly afterwards. William Weller's service was one of the best-known, with various routes east and west. Northward, there was the line run by James Mink, a black hotelier who ran a livery stable adjoining Yonge Street. One of the services northward on Yonge from 1880 to 1896 was that of John Thompson. Before that, Thompson had worked for Weller.

In this picture of the foot of Yonge Street, boats dock within yards of the Grand Trunk Railway Station on the right, and automobiles have replaced many of the horse-drawn vehicles. Comfort on the road has been improved with the introduction of rubber tires.

The earliest railways built their own facilities, but the first Union Station was constructed in 1859. Telegraph service, needed by the railways, was available to the public.

Modern Trucking Starts on Yonge

Ontario's trucking industry and the longest street in the world - Yonge Street - share a vibrant, lengthy and intertwined history. Canada's first transport truck travelled Yonge Street, and the first truck built in Canada was built on Yonge Street. Ontario's modern road network and the unfolding of the province's power-house economy were both gained by the development of the trucking industry.

In 1914, the horse was starting along the road to extinction as the servant of commerce. A progressive Toronto organization, The William Davies Company Limited, senses the onward rush to transportation progress, posed its faithful fleet of horses and the brand-new interloper (foreground). Motorized transport vehicles brought about unprecedented economic improvements – the savings that could be made by switching from horse to commercial power wagons was well known.

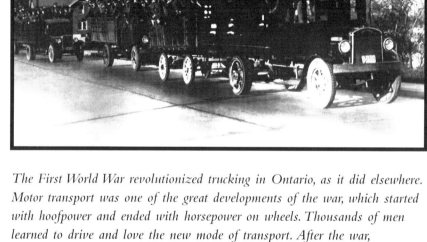

This first real electric-powered truck in Canada belonged to The Robert Simpson Co. Ltd., of Toronto who imported it in 1898. The store had been famous for years for the smart delivery wagons it used, drawn by matched gray horses. The battery truck was a big departure, yet in line with Simpson's leadership in delivery systems. The truck was built by Fisher Equipment Company of Chicago. It was supposed to have a top speed of 14 miles an hour but if it travelled at that speed on city streets it would have been breaking the law – which then limited speed to ten miles an hour. Its range was roughly 42 miles before recharging.

Less than a year after the Simpson Company purchased Canada's first commercial truck, Parker Dye Works bought an electric delivery wagon. It is of special interest because it was built in Toronto, in a factory located at Yonge Street directly across the street from Parker Dye Works.

The First World War revolutionized trucking in Ontario, as it did elsewhere. Motor transport was one of the great developments of the war, which started with hoofpower and ended with horsepower on wheels. Thousands of men learned to drive and love the new mode of transport. After the war, war-surplus trucks of many makes were available to anyone who wanted to get into trucking.

The Army seized upon the advantages of truck transport early in the game. While the French rushed the defenders of Verdun to the front in taxicabs, the Canadian Army in 1927 considered that the trucks shown here were quite satisfactory for the defenders of Canada in the peacetime years. These trucks of Martin's Transport gave the clients healthful quantities of fresh air.

Roads and Tolls

The first roads were dirt-based or of "corduroy" (logs laid across the roadbed side by side and packed with dirt) and were difficult to travel except on horseback. Wheeled vehicles provided a bone-jarring experience, and always bogged down in mud. Many overturned because of remaining tree roots and uneven surfaces. As the government had no tax base to support improvements in the earliest years, those granted lands were expected to maintain the road along their frontages. Some patents were not taken up, and some owners were absentee landlords, and others, paid for their services with additional grants, could not provide the labour. The roads remained difficult and neglected. Pathmasters were appointed to oversee the work required by the 1798 directive, and groups of landowners would assist each other under the Pathmaster's supervision. Landowners unable to contribute actual labour, could pay a fee in lieu which was used to pay others to do the work. Complaints mounted, and the government introduced tolls in the hope of generating revenue for road building. On brand-new roads, annually ravaged by spring and fall rains and by frost damage, it was nearly an impossible situation. The next phase involved the building of plank roads – a Canadian invention – which utilized the plentiful wood supply and offered smoother passage. A single plank at today's prices would be worth about $300! Macadamizing was discussed (compacting gravel into a solid mass or base) but rejected as too expensive and time-consuming. So plank roads became the standard for a number of years, and where dirt surfaces remained, efforts at eliminating ruts and ridges were made.

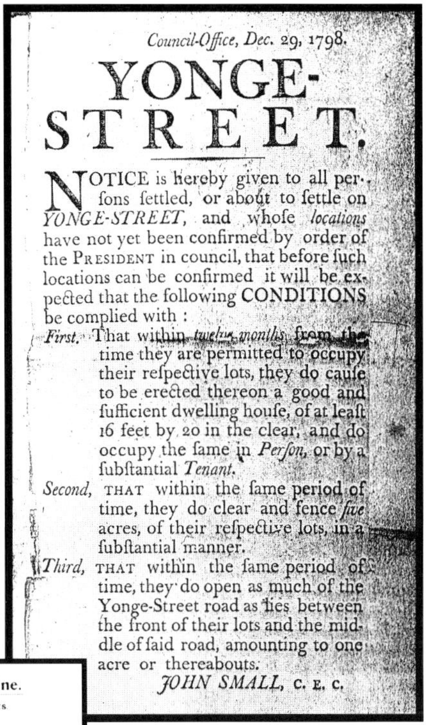

Council-Office, Dec. 29, 1798.

YONGE-STREET.

NOTICE is hereby given to all perſons ſettled, or about to ſettle on *YONGE-STREET*, and whoſe *locations* have not yet been confirmed by order of the PRESIDENT in council, that before ſuch locations can be confirmed it will be expected that the following CONDITIONS be complied with :

First, That within *twelve months* from the time they are permitted to occupy their reſpective lots, they do cauſe to be erected thereon a good and ſufficient dwelling houſe, of at leaſt 16 feet by 20 in the clear, and do occupy the ſame in *Perſon*, or by a ſubſtantial *Tenant*.

Second, THAT within the ſame period of time, they do clear and fence *five* acres, of their reſpective lots, in a ſubſtantial manner.

Third, THAT within the ſame period of time, they do open as much of the Yonge-Street road as lies between the front of their lots and the middle of ſaid road, amounting to one acre or thereabouts.

JOHN SMALL, C. E. C.

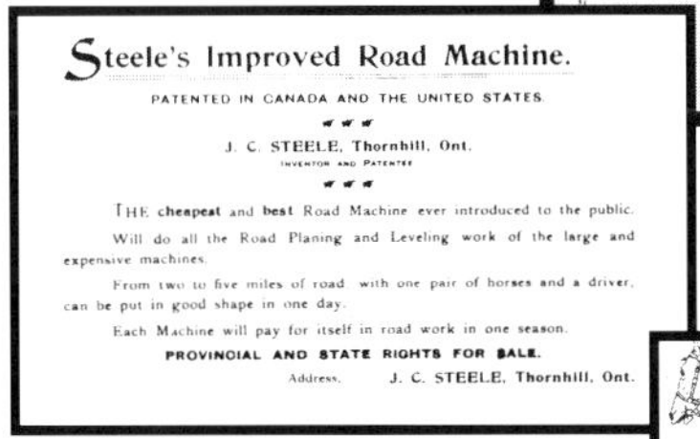

Here, in 1890, is the Langstaff Tollgate, No. 3 on Yonge. Tolls were not very successful. The plank roads lasted, at best, only ten or twelve years before the planks had to be replaced. The public resented the tolls and went to great pains to avoid them. Some companies failed to recoup their investment and went into bankruptcy. In 1894, the government abolished toll roads and took over management of intercity routes. Except for a few pictures, and one surviving tollkeeper's cottage in fragile condition, nothing remains of the era of plank and toll roads.

The Act of 13 February 1833 authorized the formation of companies to build turnpike roads, and set aside starter funding. Contracts were let by auction, with companies to build specific roads and recoup their own costs through tolls permitted at given locations. A kind of "boom" ensued, with many companies incorporating to bid on and build sections of plank roads. This picture shows No. 1 tollgate on Yonge just north of the concession road (Bloor Street), which hoped to collect from those travelling on Yonge into York, from the heavy traffic along Davenport Road diverted onto Yonge, and from Yorkvillers themselves. No. 1 was to move to locations farther north, at Davenport, then at Cottingham. This first location was opposite Potter's Field Cemetery, on the east-side lands now owned by the Hudson's Bay Company.

No. 2 tollgate on Yonge was at Hogg's Hollow, the only one with a roof over the road; No. 3 was at Cooke's Corners north of Thornhill; No. 4 was a mile and a quarter north of Elgin Mills; No. 5 was at Aurora close to the Aurora Cemetery; and No. 6 was at Cody's Corners, six and a quarter miles north of the Markham-Whitchurch Town Line.

TOWNS ALONG YONGE STREET

YORKVILLE

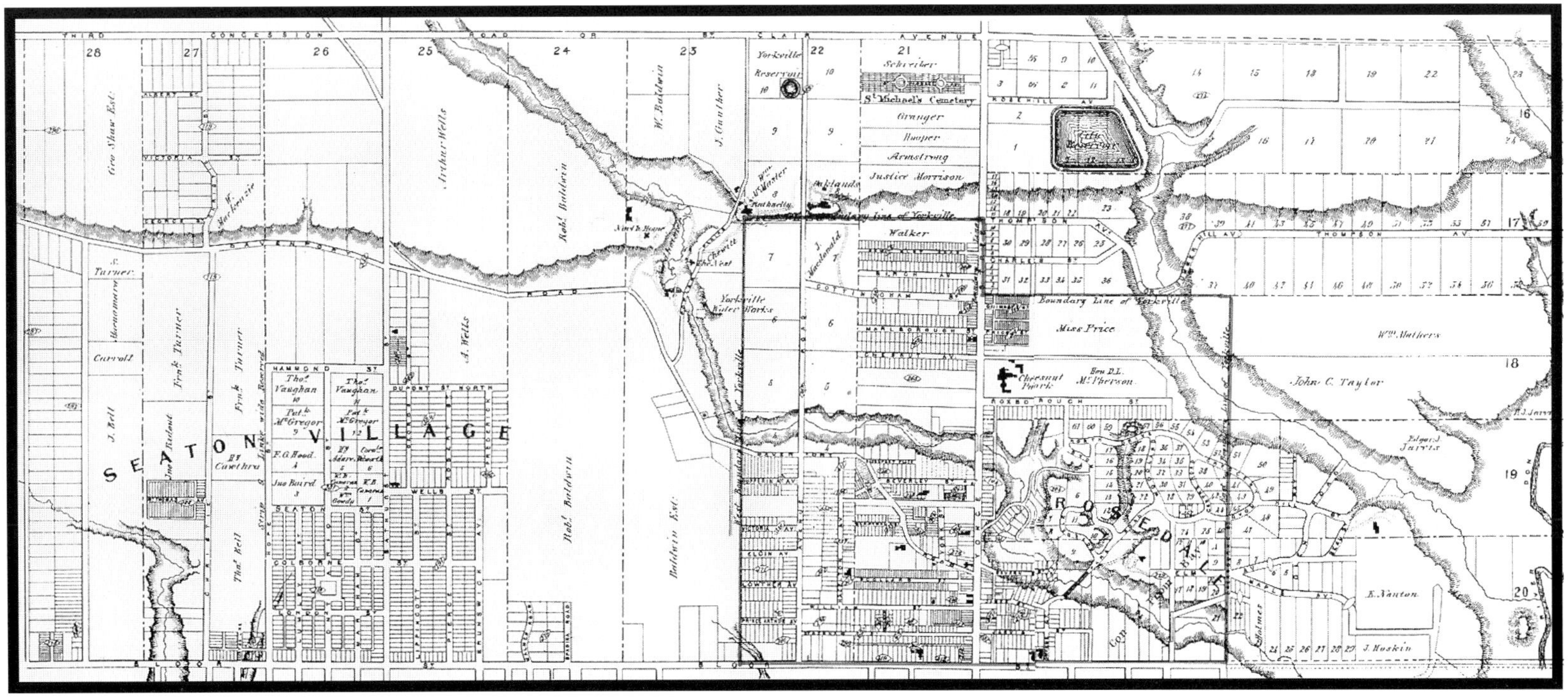

Yorkville began because Yonge Street intersected Toronto's oldest road (now called Davenport) which ran from the Humber to the Don River at the base of the escarpment crossing the city from east to west. The map shows part of Davenport as far as Yonge from the west, and eastward a portion of Castle Frank Creek – the other parts of the road and creek have been left out. On the south side of the intersection of the two roads, a large inn and stagecoach stop was built in 1808, and the village grew from this beginning, although there were earlier unidentifiable buildings and inhabitants in the area.

Davenport Road, as an aboriginal trail, is at least 10,000 years old, while the trail that Indians had made from Lake Simcoe to Lake Ontario, and which was the basis for Yonge Street, was less well-used and is less understood. But it ended at a waterfall in Castle Frank Creek where the two ancient trails met, and the lower end of the Yonge route is today known as Poplar Plains Road. Yorkville drew its water from a large pond below the waterfall at the site of today's High Level Pumping Station, pumped the water back up the escarpment to a reservoir just south of St. Clair near Avenue Road, from where it ran by gravity in pipes back to the village.

Another pond on Castle Frank Creek was larger and had laid down clay deposits over centuries which provided some of the employment for villagers. Several brickyards were located at this clay deposit and produced the "white" (actually yellow) bricks found in the remaining buildings of the 19th-century city. The other large workforce of the village was busy at either the Severn or Bloor/Castle Frank breweries which were also dependent upon Castle Frank Creek. Travellers up Yonge disliked the creek which kept the Blue Hill and Gallows Hill muddy and nearly impassable at times, making drainage and bridge-building a focus of the village council from its incorporation in 1853 until annexation in 1883.

The dream of a village was carried into reality by its first Reeve, James Dobson, a builder and the first postmaster. He bought a Lot out of farm Lot 21, laid out a subdivision, and provided space for a town hall with a market behind it. The market space was taken over later for Toronto's first public transportation line, which ran from the Town Hall to St. Lawrence Market. The village's crest was saved and may be seen on the front of the fire hall on Yorkville Avenue, but the Town Hall was lost to fire in 1945. The architect's drawings show the Town Hall, Flemish in character, with several rose windows of stained glass.

Until the 1970s, Yorkville had fine examples of every type of 19th-century architecture, from log cabins and frame cottages and farmhouses to the fine buildings of the Victorian and Edwardian periods. Yorkville even had Canada's first Jewish General Hospital to which Mount Sinai on University Avenue is the successor. Redevelopment has removed most traces of the farming community which was the first suburb of Toronto. Yonge Street was the centre of the village which once extended north of Bloor to the escarpment from near Bedford Road to Sherbourne Street – a main street which Yorkville shares with hundreds of other communities in Ontario.

Deer Park

The original Indian trail that was the basis for Yonge Street is some distance to the west of the present Yonge Street and ran through Baldwin estate lands that were not subdivided until late in the 19th century. These two sections of maps in the 1878 Miles' Atlas show Deer Park, complete with its own post office, developing on adjacent lands around the intersection of Yonge with what is now St. Clair, then a line between the Second and Third Concessions from the Bay. Never incorporated, Deer Park was a later name for a real community that had been planned first as the Town of Drummondville above St. Clair when the lands were owned by Baron Frederic de Hoen. With few people to make up a community, the plan was never realized and the Baron sold 150 acres to Mrs. Elmsley, wife of the Chief Justice, and she, in turn, sold forty acres to Mrs. Agnes Heath, a widow. Mrs. Heath settled on the land in 1837, probably near Deer Park Crescent and Heath Street West. Her son, Charles, kept deer on their farm, and the property was called Deer Park.

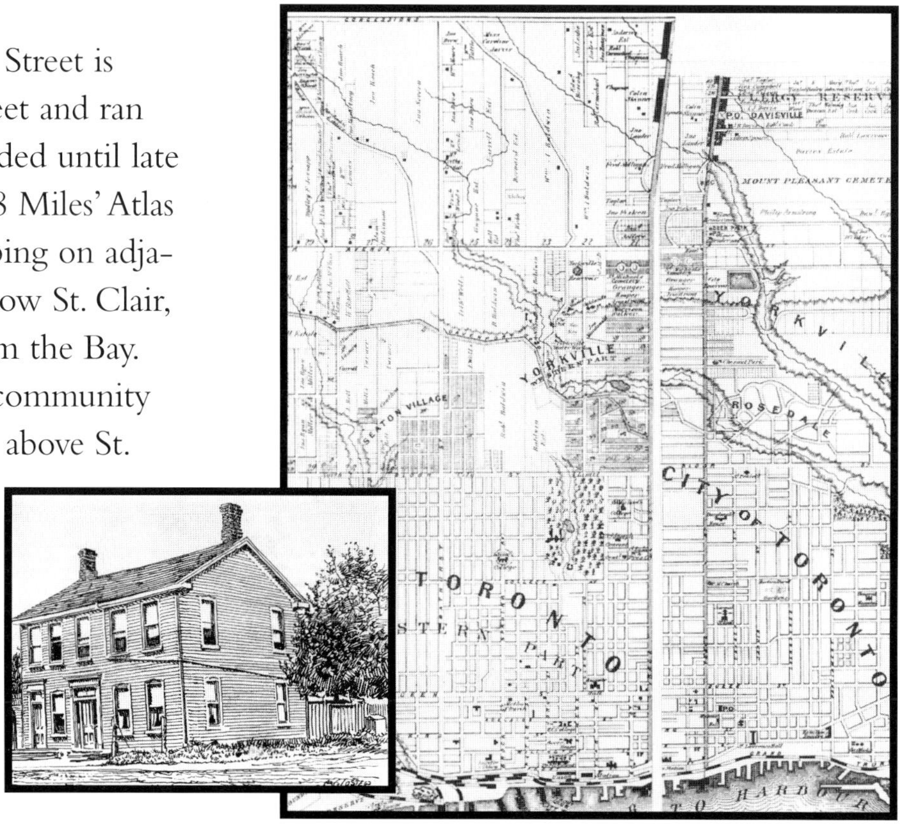

On the southwest corner of Yonge and St. Clair stood O'Halloran's Hotel, built in 1836. Deer from the Heath estate farm used to come daily to the hotel to be fed and, eventually, this custom led to a later owner renaming the hotel "Deer Park Hotel". In 1837, the rebels on Yonge used the hotel, which also served mourners from St. Michael's Cemetery to the south. South of the cemetery was a lot owned by Mr. Granger who established a florist's business lasting into the 1970s. South of Granger was the land of Mr. Hooper who founded one of the very first chains of pharmacies in Toronto. As with many Ontario communities, Deer Park grew up around the hotel, the first facility north of the escarpment.

The home of John Fisken of Deer Park shows Yonge Street above as it appeared in the 1878 Miles' Atlas. Veering westwards is "Old Yonge Street", as it was called on old maps and registered plans; today it is called Lawton Boulevard. In the triangle of land between the two is the first Christ Church Deer Park. The size of Mr. Fisken's property can be seen in the maps above, as well as the course of a creek just to the north.

A large part of this 1838 house is still standing at 35 Woodlawn Avenue West, the street named for the house, "Woodlawn". One of the oldest remaining houses in Deer Park, "Woodlawn" has been carefully preserved. Its age is noticeable because it is set far back from the modern street and has other houses built in front of it. It was built by William Hume Blake, then sold to his law partner, Joseph Curran Morrison. Blake was the first Chancellor of Ontario in 1850, and the first Solicitor General before that. His career in law and politics was brilliant. His son, Edward, married Margaret Cronyn in 1858, and completed construction of the house and some outbuildings.

Closer to Poplar Plains but listed on the present Yonge Street in early directories is Olive Grove, the home of James S. Howard, postmaster of Toronto's First Post Office after the town was incorporated. The house, long vanished, was involved in one of the incidents of the 1837 Rebellion, when William Lyon Mackenzie appeared with his rebels, demanding to be fed and granting his troops the freedom of the property. Over Mrs. Howard's strenuous objections, the men were fed. For two more days the rebels lingered, firing their guns and drinking whisky on the lawn.

City of York's Yonge Street Heritage

City of York, formerly York Township, est. 1793

As originally surveyed, the Township of York stretched from the Humber River on the west to Scarborough Township on the east, and from Lake Ontario in the south to the Townships of Vaughan and Markham in the north. When Yonge Street was surveyed and built between 1793 and 1796, the portion of it located within the Township of York stretched continuously for ten miles from Queen Street to Steeles Avenue. Yonge Street was the first concession line for York Township, and the Base Line for Side Roads would become known as Eglinton Avenue.

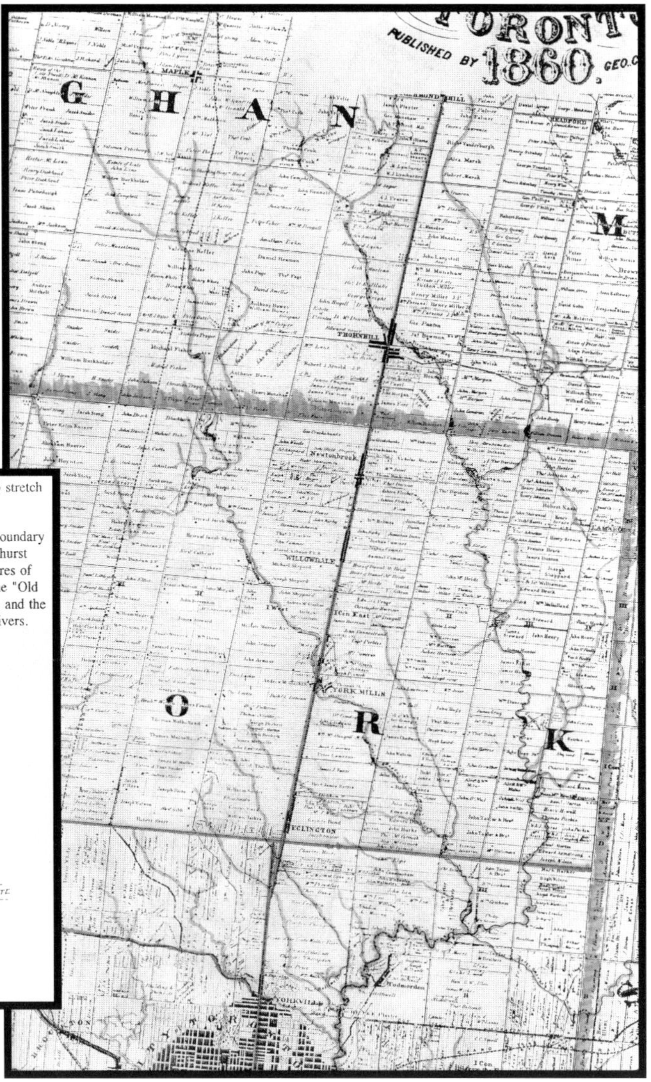

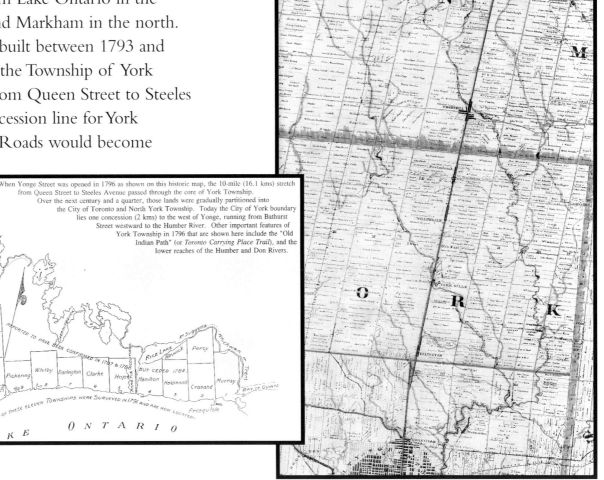

When Yonge Street was opened in 1796 as shown on this historic map, the 10-mile (16.1 kms) stretch from Queen Street to Steeles Avenue passed through the core of York Township. Over the next century and a quarter, those lands were gradually partitioned into the City of Toronto and North York Township. Today the City of York boundary lies one concession (2 kms) to the west of Yonge, running from Bathurst Street westward to the Humber River. Other important features of York Township in 1796 that are shown here include the "Old Indian Path" (or *Toronto Carrying Place Trail*), and the lower reaches of the Humber and Don Rivers.

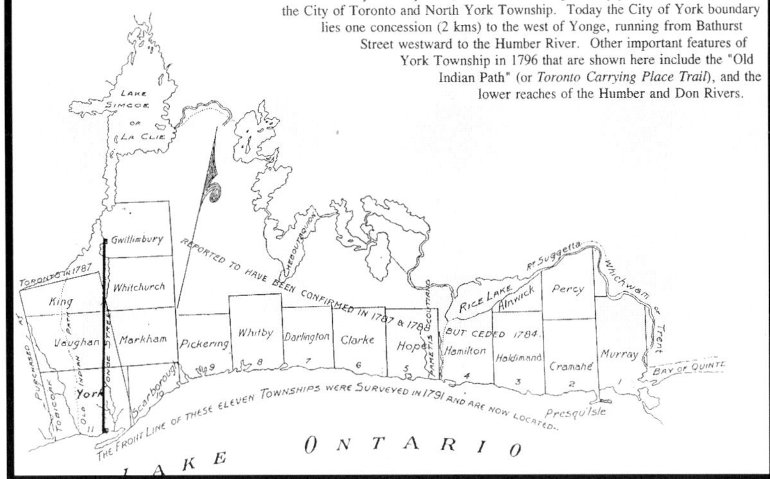

PLANK ROAD BUILDING
2371 Weston Road

Another important link the City of York has with Yonge Street is the Davenport Trail. This trail marks the route used for thousands of years by native peoples between the Humber and Don Rivers. Villages became established along Davenport which is Toronto's oldest road. The Davenport trail links up with Weston Road which was also the Toronto Carrying Place Trail earlier (the trail that gave Toronto its name) and this trail is a portage route up the Humber/Holland River system. The Toronto Carrying Place Trail was used by Governor Simcoe to reach Lake Simcoe, and he returned by means of the trail that became the route for Yonge Street. Historically designated by the City of York, the Weston Plank Road Building was the office for the company which built wooden plank toll roads as far north as the villages of Albion and Woodbridge.

LAMBTON HOUSE

near the Humber River on the Davenport Trail

Restored in 1993 for the City of York Bicentennial, the house was opened by Lieutenant-Governor H. Jackman. The inn was originally owned by Sir William P. Howland who was the first Lieutenant-Governor after Confederation.

LAMBTON HOUSE

near the Humber River on Dundas Street

In its original form, the inn was used as a stopover on the stagecoach route along Dundas Street (Highway 5) from Toronto west to Dundas (Hamilton) and continued west to London, Ontario. The picture was taken around Confederation.

TURNING LOOP FOR LAMBTON ELECTRIC STREET RAILWAY (LEFT)

In conjunction with the mill dam at Lambton, Howland established a hydro-electric station in the 1880s which powered the street railway that travelled between Lambton Mills and West Toronto Junction, there linking with what became the TTC, Dundas line, to Yonge Street. The hydro station also provided Lambton Mills with electric lighting before the turn of the century.

HOWLAND GRIST MILL (RIGHT) *c. 1890s*

The Howland brothers owned three mills: a woolen mill, a grist mill, and a saw mill. Located at Lambton Mills, they supported a distillery, an office, a hotel, a general store and post office. The grist mill produced enough flour to require two teams of horses per day to haul flour into Toronto, and it drew grain from a forty-mile radius. They used the Humber River and Davenport Trail to get flour to Yonge Street. Lambton Mills was officially named Lambton in 1851, with a population of about 100. W.P. Howland became a member of the legislature for the area in the 1840s and a Father of Confederation at Charlottetown. Two of his sons became Mayors of Toronto. Lambton Mills was an important junction in York Township as all traffic coming from St. Clair, Davenport, and Dundas had to pass through Lambton to cross York's western boundary, the Humber River. Originally an aboriginal fording point, replaced by a succession of bridges, Lambton Mills was typical of all the little villages like Davisville and Eglinton which evolved early and quickly because of their location on the Humber route and early trails and roads, and because of the source of waterpower in the Humber. The probable architect of Lambton House was Squire William Tyrrell, a friend of Howland, Mayor of Weston and Reeve of York Township. Tyrrell designed homes, mills, bridges, and sewer systems throughout the Humber valley and Toronto area.

Howland Mill office c. 1890s

Yonge Street was in York Township as an Indian trail when Augustus Jones first surveyed it for Simcoe and when he later married a Mississauga woman from the Humber. Yonge Street was in York Township when the Home District Council (York City Council) met in offices over the Sheppard store at Yonge and Sheppard Avenue – the store known later as Dempsey Brothers Hardware (See page 115). Yonge Street was still in York Township when the York County League of Women Voters was formed - a powerful policy group for several decades. York Township, the City of York, and life in the Humber region are still linked in many ways to Yonge Street.

North Toronto

DAVISVILLE GENERAL STORE AND POST OFFICE *c.1905*

1909 Yonge, northeast corner of Davisville Avenue

J.J. (Jack) Davis, grandson of potter John Davis, a founder of Davisville, operated a general store and post office from this location. The building which until recently was known as the "Curiosity Shop", is on the Toronto Historical Board's Inventory of Heritage Properties.

OULCOTT'S HOTEL AND NORTH TORONTO TOWN HALL

Yonge Street west side at Montgomery Avenue, c.1905

John Oulcott opened this hotel (on the site of the former Montgomery's Tavern of 1837 Rebellion fame) in 1883. It was a three-storey building with extensive driving sheds and stables. By 1923, it was no longer a hotel, but was used as the North Toronto Post Office. The building was demolished and replaced by Postal Station K in 1936. To the north in this photo is the North Toronto Town Hall, designed by the architectural firm of Langley, Langley and Burke and built by the local builders Fisher and Ramsay. North Toronto was a separate municipality from 1889 to 1912 when it was annexed to the City of Toronto. The building was demolished and replaced by Police Station #12 in 1932.

2084 - 2090 YONGE STREET, *November 21, 1921*
west side, near Manor Road

These workers' cottages, long since gone, are a reminder of some of the modest dwellings which once fronted Yonge Street in this area.

J. ATKINSON & SONS STORE *c. 1920*

3160-3164 Yonge at southwest corner with Bedford Park Avenue

John Atkinson moved to this location from his store at Lawrence and Yonge in 1898. Atkinson's was a general store selling clothing and food as well as hardware, and was also the location of the Bedford Park Post Office. Before the building was sold in 1956, it was run by John Atkinson's sons Harry and Gordon. Today, the building houses dental offices. It is listed on the Toronto Historical Board's Inventory of Heritage Properties.

CONSUMERS GAS COMPANY, *1931*

Yonge Street at St. Clements Avenue

This handsome building, incorporating granite, cut stone, and exterior marble as well as decorative aluminum, was designed by architect Charles Dolphin. It included modern appliance salesrooms and a home demonstration auditorium on the second floor and opened to the public in January 1931. The building has been designated for its architecture and now operates as the Childrens Book Store.

YONGE STREET AT GLENGROVE AVENUE, *1898*

Glengrove was the northern limit for the five-cent fare on the Metropolitan Street Railway of the Toronto line; through cars to Richmond Hill continued north from this point. The small building on the left is the passengers' shelter. Adjacent, the Glen Grove Racetrack can be seen through the pine trees at left.

NORTH YORK

NEWTONBROOK: *Manse for Newtonbrook United Church. Birthplace of Prime Minister Lester B. Pearson. (Approx 1906-1910)*

WILLOWDALE: *Yonge Street looking north from Joe Smith's. Near Yonge and Church.*

NEWTONBROOK: *Highway #11, breaking up macadam road.*

NEWTONBROOK: *Lot 26, Conc. 1W. Yonge Street looking north at Steeles Corners. Green Bush Inn.*

YORK MILLS: *Lot 13, Conc. 1W. This is a view of the valley on the west side of Yonge Street. The grist flour mill was originally built by Cornelius van Nostrand in 1837. It was the upper mill of the York Hill Steam Mills, and there was also a sawmill and distiller very near to it.*

YORK MILLS: *Yonge Street looking north from York Mills Bridge (1920).*

WILLOWDALE: *Lot 18, Conc. 1W. Gibson House, Yonge Street, built 1849-51. Peter Gibson left of front steps. (c1870)*

LANSING: *Yonge Street at Sheppard Avenue looking north. (Approx 1911)*

WILLOWDALE: *Willowdale Episcopal Methodist Church parsonage, on Yonge Street, west side, just north of Gibson House.*

RICHMOND HILL

Richmond Hill, strategically located on Yonge Street, was a natural stopping place for travellers going north. Yonge was the division line between the townships of Markham and Vaughan. Evolving into a farming and trade centre, its population at the time of incorporation as a village in 1873 was 631. It became a town in 1957. In 1971, parts of neighbouring communities were annexed and Richmond Hill became part of the Region of York. Today, with a population of over 100,000 people, Richmond Hill is one of Canada's fastest growing communities, a reflection of the significant role Yonge Street played in the development of Richmond Hill.

The Metropolitan Railway Station, circa 1909, on the northeast corner of Yonge and Lorne Avenue. It was demolished in 1952 and a Bank of Nova Scotia was built on the site. The radial car operated on Yonge from 1897 to 1948 when it was replaced by buses.

A team and wagon at Tollgate #3, the Langstaff Tollgate, located once where Yonge Street and today's Highway No.7 intersect. The tollgates were let by auction annually. Travelling down Yonge was the most convenient way to reach the York Farmers' Market (St. Lawrence Market). At first, the profits which the gatekeeper could keep were considerable, then costs mounted. It was in 1845 when this tollgate was let to Leonard Klinck.

Top: The first stagecoach service was operated by George Playter & Son, and could carry eight to nine passengers inside with two sitting along with the driver. In 1840, Charles Thompson started his well-known stagecoach line, with a fare of 75¢ from Richmond Hill to York (St. Lawrence) Market.

Above: The corner of Yonge and Major Mackenzie Drive has seen many changes. The needs of 19th-century travellers were served by Abner Miles' tavern and store on the southeast corner – the beginning of Richmond Hill's hospitality industry – while across the road Miles ran a potash business. The west side of the intersection had the Anglican and Presbyterian churches. Church spires have always been a feature of Richmond Hill's skyline.

The Elgin Mills Hotel on Yonge Street looking north from Elgin Mills Road, in the 1920's. Elgin Mills was once a distinct community, quite separate from its southern neighbour, Richmond Hill. It was here that the first settler of Richmond Hill, Balsar Munshaw, took up land. The Munshaw's daughter, Susan, was the first white child born in the Township of Vaughan and the first on Yonge Street. After a short stay at Elgin Mills they moved to Lot 35, Markham, just to the south.

AURORA

LANDMARKS IN AURORA'S HISTORY

1796 Yonge Street opened, providing impetus for settlement of what will become Aurora

1797 First patents granted in Aurora area of King and Whitchurch Townships

1834 Name "Machell's Corners" informally adopted, after owner of general store at Yonge/Wellington crossroads

1846 First post office, "Whitchurch", opened

1853 Ontario, Simcoe and Huron Union Railroad arrived

1854 Post office name changed to "Aurora"

1863 Incorporation as a village straddling Yonge Street with same name as post office

1888 Incorporation as a town

1899 Radial railway arrived

1957 Announcement of Sterling Drug plant and first homes in Aurora Heights subdivision mark beginning of period of Aurora's greatest growth

1971 Major expansion of boundaries as town becomes an area municipality within the Regional Municipality of York

Yonge Street, Aurora, looking north from near Tyler Street in the early 1700s. The road would not be paved for decades yet, but board sidewalks and crossing places were provided. Nearly all the buildings visible have since been demolished, or were victims to fire, but three do survive.

Looking north from just south of Mosley Street, about 1905. Many of the buildings of the 1870's have already been replaced, or clad with brick for greater dignity – and fire resistance. Yonge Street is still muddy, but it carries the tracks of the electrical radial railway, which had reached Aurora in 1899.

By the 1940's, as shown in this view, the automobile had begun to show signs of the dominance it would one day have. The radial railway tracks were taken up in 1930: the line could not compete with the convenience of the car and truck.

YONGE STREET: THE HISTORIC HEART OF AURORA

The Aurora Dairy, built in 1938, typified the clean-cut architecture of its decade, with a few Art Deco touches. It was built on the site of an old dwelling, and was itself replaced in 1984.

When Yonge Street was still the major route to the north, the Queen's Hotel was a favourite stopping place for travellers. Additions in the 1930s hid the elegance of the 1860s building, and it was a sad reminder of its former self when demolished in 1971.

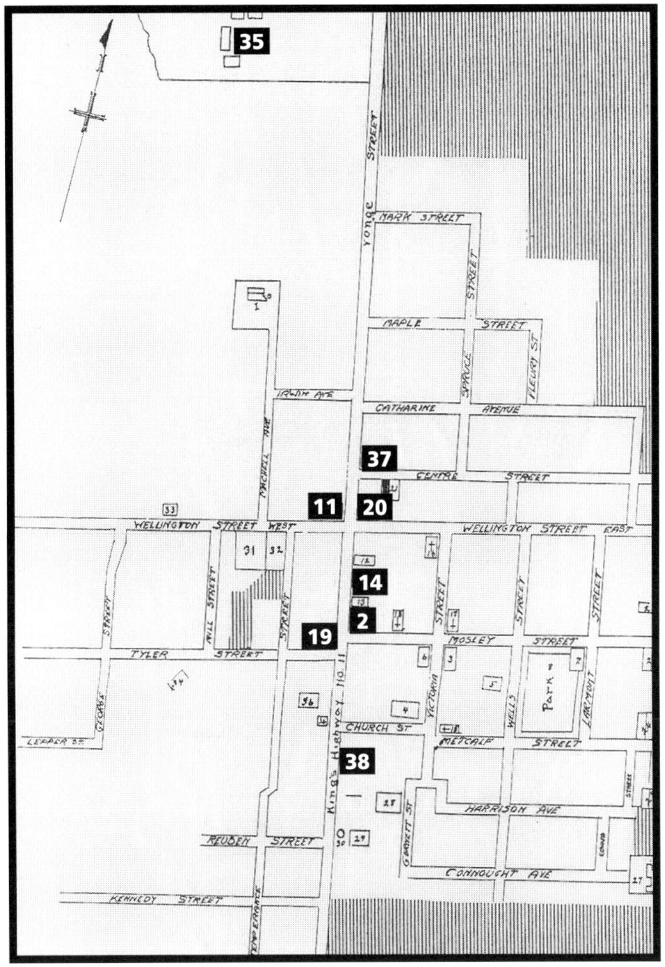

Map from a 1940s promotional brochure. Of the buildings illustrated, only St Andrew's College, the post office, and the United Church survive.

St Andrew's College, an independent school for boys, moved from Toronto to Aurora in 1926. Shown here on a postcard from the 1950's, it has since expanded so as to combine time-honoured values with up-to-date educational facilities.

Since 1888 the Bank of Montreal (and its predecessor, the Ontario Bank) has anchored the north-west corner of Yonge and Wellington streets. The building shown, erected in 1922, was in the dignified classical style thought appropriate for banks at that time. This building was replaced in 1973.

There has been a church building on this corner since 1818; the 1874 structure shown here was the third on the site. It still stands as a Yonge Street landmark – without its spires – and is the oldest church building in town still used as a church. Rev. Edwin A. Pearson, father of future prime minister Lester B. Pearson, was minister here from 1900 to 1903.

The Italianate style of Aurora's post office, shown here at the time of its 1914 construction, is similar to others of that era across Canada. Typical, too, was its importance as a central gathering point. Today the building is privately owned, but its clock still services the town well.

Aurora's first purpose-built town hall, designed by Langley, Langley, and Burke, accommodated a market, the fire station, a public hall, and the lock-up in addition to the municipal offices when it was opened in 1876. This photo dates from about 1950; the building was demolished in 1956.

For many travellers to the vacation country in the north, Aurora's Cousins Dairy was famous for its ice cream. Seen here in the 1930's, Cousins had as its neighbour the Bell Telephone exchange and office. These very similar buildings, erected in the 1920's, have both now disappeared.

Newmarket

EARLY DEVELOPMENT AROUND NORTH YONGE

In 1801, the Quaker settlers built a small log meeting house on the northeast corner of Yonge and Eagle Streets. A miller, Joseph Hill, a Quaker, dammed the river near the ford where Timothy Rogers had originally rested on his first journey to York Region. By damming the river, he created a millpond known today as Fairy Lake. By the week before Christmas 1801, he had ground his first bushel of wheat in the primitive mill with a run of two stones that Timothy Rogers must have helped him construct. Hill also built a store and a frame house (seen on the right). Hill's lonely forest clearing offered an alternate trading post, a new market, cutting off the arduous portage over the Oak Ridges and down to muddy York for trappers, Indians, and settlers from the north.

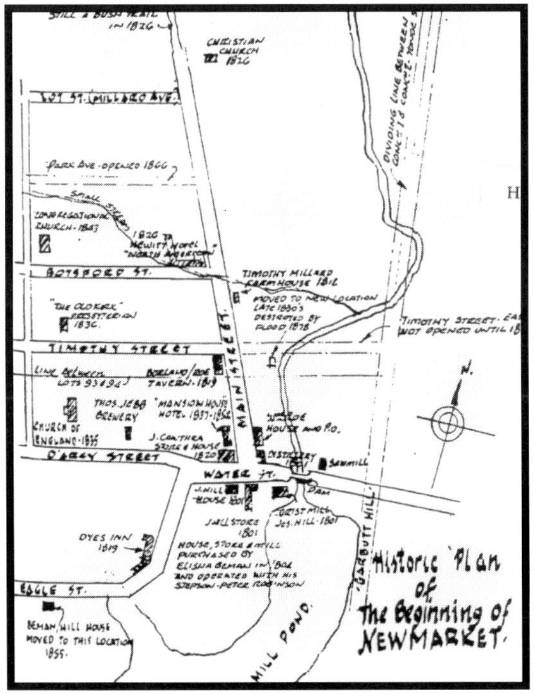

Historic plan of beginning Newmarket.

BEGINNING OF THE TOWN OF NEWMARKET

In March 1812, it is recorded that Timothy Millard purchased lot 94, comprising 200 acres, from Timothy Rogers. This farm extended from Yonge Street to the 2nd Concession, with the southern boundary just south of Timothy Street, and the northern boundary near Queen Street. Timothy Street was named after Timothy Millard. At the east end of his farm on the east side of the Indian Trail (Main Street), he erected his farm house, which was the second frame house built in Newmarket, prior to 1814. There were some log houses built earlier.

THE JOSEPH HILL–ELISHA BEMAN HOUSE

Built by Joseph Hill in 1801 and later occupied by Elisha Beman, this is the oldest building in Newmarket of which remnants remain. Above, a pen and ink sketch of the original house by George Luesby. Below, a photograph of the log house covered by siding on its present site at Eagle and Church Streets.

Right: Circa 1910, looking north on Main Street in Newmarket.

Circa 1915-20, looking north on Main Street in Newmarket.

PRESENT DAY TOWN OF NEWMARKET

Right: This is a portion of a brochure produced by George Luesby, town historian, to show the relationship of Newmarket to Yonge Street, as well as historical houses along Yonge. Since this was produced, the Sarah Rogers house has been demolished; the York Manor has been demolished to produce a park in front of the new Regional building; the George Dawson house has been moved; Bonshaw has been moved; and the Benjamin Cody house has been demolished. Development has come to Yonge Street as it changes to the northern commercial hub of York Region.

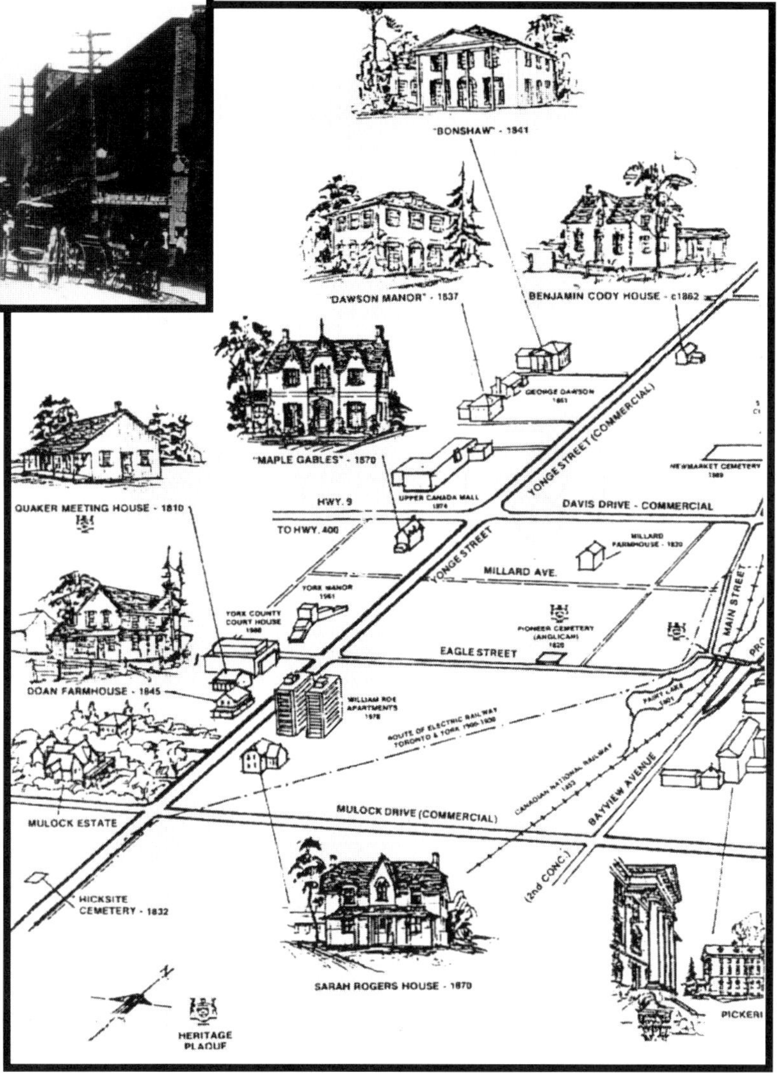

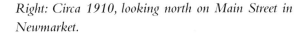

THE QUAKERS

Timothy Rogers arrived near the location of present-day Newmarket in 1800. This Vermont wheelwright was on a trip to relocate his family and a group of Quaker settlers on good land on the new frontier. He was also responding to Governor Simcoe's offer of free land in York County. He made his first camp on the Indian Trail beside the East Holland River; this Trail was destined to become the Main Street of Newmarket. Rogers returned to Pennsylvania and New England and convinced forty families to return with him to north Yonge Street in the winter of 1800. Soon after, he received a grant of forty farms of 200 acres each, and Samuel Lundy came from Pennsylvania to take adjoining land, receiving land for another twenty families. The Quakers took very seriously the job of clearing and maintaining the road in front of their farms. In early 1800, reports on the progress of Yonge Street noted that their section was one of the earliest built and best maintained.

QUAKER MEETING HOUSE

Shown before (inset), and after (above) restoration in 1976, this meeting house was built in 1810 on land deeded by Asa Rogers and William Doan, and was the first permanent place of worship erected north of Toronto. It is still used today. Many of the early settlers and their descendants are buried in the adjoining cemetery

The ambrotype opposite shows Main Street in 1856 and is one of the earliest pictures of Main Street. The North American Hotel is numbers 5 and 6. Other buildings were businesses and homes.

TRAVELLING BY STAGECOACH ALONG YONGE

In 1826, Captain James Hewitt built the North American Hotel on Main Street in Newmarket. This establishment was to make a name among frontier travellers as the headquarters for the four-horse mail and stagecoaches running up Yonge from Toronto to Holland Landing. Hewitt became a partner in the stagecoach company, a profitable business until the arrival of the railway in 1853. The coach travelled from tavern to tavern.

DAWSON MANOR

Built in 1837 on lot 97 west side of Yonge north of Davis Drive by John Dawson, a medical doctor from Yorkshire, England, was lived in for generations by the family. In 1995, the property was sold to a developer who replaced it with a Canadian Tire store and moved the house about 1000 yards into a subdivision.

BONSHAW

Was built in 1841 on lot 98 on the west side of Yonge street, just north of Davis Drive, by Jacob Aemilius Irving from Dumfries, Scotland. It remained in the Irving family until the 1950s when it was sold to a developer. Once surrounded by tall trees and hedges which have been stripped away, the house has been moved back 1000 yards into a subdivision with Dawson Manor, to make space for a large retail store, Home Depot.

Green Lane

100	Ephraim Talbot 1804	H. Proctor 1855
99	Wm Phillips 1805	Theodoer Wine 1804
98	Bethnel Huntley 1805	Obadiah Griffin 1805
97	Nathanial Gager 1805	Thomas Young 1803
56	Obadiah Rogers 1835 Davis Dr.	Nehemiah Hide 1804
95	Jas Rogers 1804	Timothy Rogers 1804
94	Ning Rogers 1805	Henry Crone 1804
93	Isaac Rogers 1805	Jan McMurty 1802
92	Asa Rogers 1804	Simon McMirty 1802
91	Rufus Rogers 1804 Mulock Dr.	Stephen Barbace 1802
90	Nathanial Gamble 1802	Nathanial Hastings 1807
89	Isaac Phillips 1802	Nathanial Gamble Sr. 1802
88	Isaac Hollingshead 1803	Andrew Clubine 1805?
87	Jas Gilbert 1802	Jas Miles 1803?
86	Benjamin Pearson 1860 St. John's Side Road	Robert Ward 1805

Bathurst St. · Yonge St. · Bayview Ave.

Original settlers on properties 86 to 100 (present day Newmarket) in the 1st Concessions east and west of Yonge, circa 1804, adapted from the Historical Atlas of York County 1878 by Miles.

DOAN FARMHOUSE

Built in 1845 on lot 92, west side of Yonge Street south of Eagle Street, by William Doan who emigrated from Bucks County, Pennsylvania and purchased 200 acres from Asa Rogers in 1807. It was held by the Doan family until 1967 when it was bought by a developer who now uses it as an office until development begins.

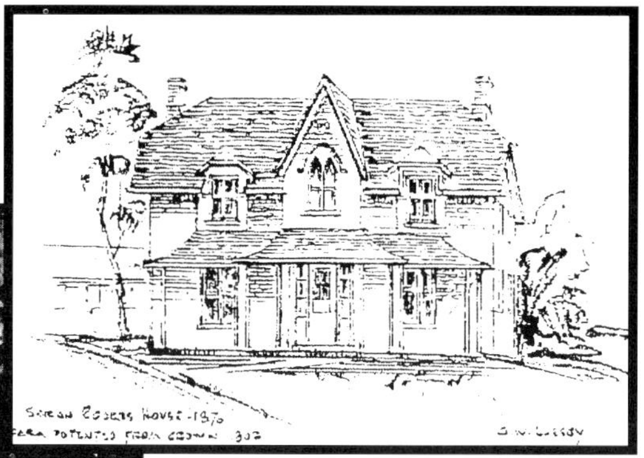

SARAH ROGERS HOUSE

Was built on lot 91 on the east side of Yonge north of Mulock. The lot was patented in 1802. This house replaced an original two-storey frame dwelling designed by John T. Stokes which was destroyed by fire, but the second house too was destroyed in the early 1990s to provide space for townhouses.

Holland Landing

A BRIEF HISTORY OF HOLLAND LANDING IN EAST GWILLIMBURY

Two hundred years ago on February 16, 1796, Holland Landing became the northern terminus of Yonge Street.

Early maps by French cartographers (1674-5) reveal the first reference to a portage or communication route which played perhaps the most significant role in the early development of the East Gwillimbury region.

There were several trails from Lake Ontario to the Holland River, frequented by the first inhabitants of the area and by the tribes who followed them, both before and after 1615. The Upper Landing was, for centuries, the ancient Indian place of embarkation situated at the north end of the Rouge-Holland and Humber-Holland portage.

In 1793, Governor Simcoe's discovery of the east branch of the Holland River resulted in the plan for Yonge Street. Simcoe believed it would be an ideal shipping and defense point between York and the British naval posts of Georgian Bay. He named the Holland River after a former Surveyor-General of Canada, Major Samuel Holland, who explored the country in 1791.

In December 1795, Governor Simcoe directed surveyor Augustus Jones to survey and open a cart road from York to the Pine Fort at the Upper Landing. The site of the Pine Fort was called Gwillimbury after Mrs. Simcoe's father, Major Gwillim. Surveyor Augustus Jones began his line at Lot 111, 33 miles and 53 chains from York. A party of Queen's York Rangers were engaged in the work and the road was blazed in about six weeks. On February 20, 1796 Augustus Jones went to York and waited on Governor Simcoe to inform him that Yonge Street was opened from York to the Pine Fort Landing, Lake Simcoe.

Built in 1840 at the corner of Yonge Street and Bradford Road, this property was purchased by James McClure in 1869 and operated as a hotel until 1901.

The North West Company chose Yonge Street as a fur trading route to the Upper Lakes and the West about 1799. The fur trade was chiefly supplied from the Great Lakes and the Indians, canoeing up the Holland River in the spring with their furs, would set up 30 to 40 large wigwams on the commons adjoining the landing place. Around this, a small by-town consisting of two or three business places arose in the 1820s. The Upper Landing was frequently called Johnson's Landing, after Joseph Johnson its first settler, who built an inn, a large log dwelling which still stands on Lot 111 today. This area also became known as Beverly in honour of Peter Robinson's brother, John Beverly Robinson. The cluster of buildings at the bottom of the hill was named St Alban's after a town in Hertfordshire,

Christ Church (Anglican) stands on a hill on the east side of Yonge Street. It was erected in 1843 on land donated by Chief Justice John Robinson. The plan of the church, built by architect John G. Howard, is similar to St John's York Mills.

England. When the Post Office was established in 1821, the name was officially changed to Holland Landing.

Just south of the Upper Landing, Peter Robinson bought the John Eave's sawmill, the village's first, and built the Red Mills nearby. A few years later, he also built a large inn south of and near the Red Mills, which he leased to Francis Phelps as a tavern. Throughout the 1830s and 40s growth occurred steadily around the mills and tavern in the form of new industries such as a brewery, distillery, tannery, foundry and other grist, flour and woolen mills. Holland Landing was the county seat of Simcoe from 1821 until 1837, when Barrie succeeded it. It was the main gateway to Simcoe Country and, in 1852, Holland Landing was annexed by York County.

The Lower Landing located on Lot 118 is the first landing south of Lake Simcoe to be encountered after entering the East Holland River. It has been referred to as the Old Indian Landing and was regularly used during the War of 1812, as it was the farthest place up the Holland River that could be reached by bateau, being 25 yards wide at this point. As settlement spread northward, bateau and raft were invaluable to the first inhabitants travelling between Holland Landing and Barrie on Lake Simcoe. The appearance of the first steamboats and stage wagons in the 1830s brought increased river and road traffic through the village. In 1832, the first steamboat, *The Simcoe* was built, followed by *The Peter Robinson*, which was launched at Holland Landing in 1833. Peter Robinson continued to play an active role in the appearance of the village when he laid out a town plot along Yonge Street. The bustling activity on Yonge Street and the Holland River, along with the building of the new railway, made Holland Landing the busiest centre in the watershed by 1853. Although the population grew to an estimated 700 by 1873, the advent of the railway brought a decline in the village's growth rate with only a handful of small businesses by the end of the nineteenth century. For much of the early 1900s, the rural community grew smaller in population and importance. This was partly due to the deviation of New Yonge Street, just below the village, which by-passed Holland Landing altogether.

Many signs of the town's part still remain today including the old canal locks, the Anglican and United Churches, the Joseph Johnson and Peter Robinson Inns, the Royal Hotel and the Holland Landing Anchor. This four-thousand pound anchor, forged in England, was being transported by sleigh along Yonge Street from York enroute to the naval post at Penetang. When the Peace treaty between Britain and United States was signed in 1815, the anchor was abandoned near Lot 116 at Soldier's Bay. It now rests at Anchor Park.

In 1933, Holland Landing ceased to be an organized village and became part of Gwillimbury East Township. With the introduction of Regional Government in 1971, it became part of the Town of East Gwillimbury in York Region.

Situated on the west side of Yonge Street, north of "Holland Court", this is one of the few remaining houses from the early village years. At one time, it was owned by John Tate, blacksmith.

The Royal Hotel, Yonge and School Streets, was owned and operated by Thomas May from the early 1840s until 1855 – the largest and best hotel in the village.

Above: Holland Landing looking south toward the site of the Eave's Sawmill of 1811 and the Red Mills built by Peter Robinson in 1821. All traces of the mill sites were lost due to the canal works in 1906.

Right: Joseph Johnson Inn, circa 1820, built on the Gwillimbury Town Plot at the Upper Landing, on Lot 111, Yonge Street.

Immediately north of the canal at Yonge and Queen Street are a pair of houses on the west side known as "Holland Court". These buildings were built in 1870 and were said to have been used as a court house at one time.

A sturdy stone foundation supports this house built by William J. Sloane in 1836, with parapeted gabled ends and date stone. It is situated south of the canal and north of the railway, east of Yonge Street.

Remains of the Holland River Canal and Locks, Lot 106, Yonge Street, proposed in 1841 and constructed between 1906 and 1911 when construction was halted.

Bradford West Gwillimbury

Explorations began in this area immediately after the passing of the Constitutional Act of 1791, dividing Canada into Upper and Lower provinces. The government of Upper Canada sent Major S. Holland, a surveyor and explorer, into the wilds of York County. He arrived first at the east branch of the river that bears his name and laid out a small settlement of log cabins. Then he travelled down the east branch to the main river and back to Lake Simcoe via the west branch. Lake Simcoe and Simcoe County were named for the first Lieutenant-Governor of the province, John Graves Simcoe, whose term of office, 1791-1797, marked the earliest period of exploration in the area after the French Regime. The Township of West Gwillimbury takes its name from the maiden name of Simcoe's wife, Elizabeth Posthuma Gwillim; "bury" is a contraction of "borough". Bradford was named after its counterpart in England, and was incorporated in 1853 with a population of about 1000. The town and township amalgamated in 1991 to form Bradford West Gwillimbury.

The town was born when William Milloy moved from Coulson's Hill and built a tavern out of logs at the forks of the road, where a branch ran north to the Scotch Settlement. The tavern at that fork was almost directly north of the town hall. But a year later, a surveyor, probably Holland, laid out Holland, Barrie, John and Colborne Streets, changed the route of the road and isolated the tavern. Another tavern, built in 1831 or 1832 by John Edmanson, was located near the fork of Barrie Street and the Scotch Line. Later, it became the Bingham Hotel. Its construction marked the beginning of an influx of new residents, many of whom bought lots from an enterprising lady, Miss Letitia Magee, who had already acquired the block from Holland and Barrie Streets up to the next concession. In the meantime, William Milloy, done out of business at his first location, crossed the river and built a hostelry in the 1830s. Local people dubbed it the "Bullfrog Tavern" and, during the 1837 Rebellion, a hundred or more soldiers were quartered there. The lands around the tavern had been surveyed in 1836 by George Lount, who laid out streets with Dutch names and called the area Amsterdam.

Barrie Street, Bradford, as it was.

EARLY WEST GWILLIMBURY SETTLERS

Before any buildings existed in Bradford, there were little settlements in the Township of West Gwillimbury. The first to cross the Holland River were three Irishmen, James Wallace, Lewis Algeo, and Robert Armstrong, who settled on concessions 6 and 7 in 1819.

Soon after, came a party of Selkirk Settlers who formed the "Scotch Settlement"; these settlers had come from the tragic settlement on the Red River through the wilderness to Fort William on Lake Superior and then by Northwest Company boats to the Nottawasaga River, a portage, to Lake Simcoe and the Holland River. In 1821, they arrived at the third concession where they established themselves. The next year, they began a Presbyterian congregation and by 1823 had built a log church and schoolhouse.

North of Bradford, the earliest settlers were Irish and, as early as 1824, Mark Scanlon and John Thorpe were operating a mill on Scanlon's Creek. As many as six mills were in operation at one time on that creek, and some of the millers were Mr Mackie, Mr Wood, Enos Rogers, and Zachariah Evans. This area was so busy that a station was established there when the railroads came. Albert Scanlon, grandson of Mark, served as Bradford's Reeve for many years and as Warden of Simcoe County.

Further north, Coulson's Hill derived its name from John Coulson, as did Fennells from Joseph Fennell, J.P., who settled there about 1831. Four members of the Kneeshaw family settled west of Coulson's on concession 11 in the 1820s. James Tindall settled in the Ebenezer district in 1830 and is credited with promoting the Ebenezer Church at Deerhurst. John Garbutt was an 1823 settler in The Hollows. In the Gilford district many settlers in the 1830s were Irish and their names are still prominent in the community: Neilly, Gibbons, Bell, Sawyer, O'Donnell, Doolittle, Dillon, Rothwell, and Roberts.

Along the Bond Head Road, John Stoddary and his three sons settled in 1829, and, further along the road, William Armson became West Gwillimbury's first Reeve and first Warden of Simcoe County in 1846. The history of the Bond Head is especially rich and includes the ancestors of the Osler and Mulock families that became world-famous. Bond Head was a major business centre in the days of plank roads. Latimer's Corners, pioneered by Thomas and Henry Matchett, Isaiah Rogers and John Lee, was later renamed Newton Robinson.

The Plank Road had been built from Bradford to Bond Head and from Bradford to Holland Landing in 1852. The picture above shows the tollgate, south of the river on Yonge Street. Other tolls were set up at Middleton and south of the river. The lines of grain-loaded wagons on Bradford's streets at times were so long that they reached north of Bond Head. The Plank Road's route can be traced in sections of Highway 11 and also Highway 88.

In 1824, settlers in West Gwillimbury petitioned the government of Upper Canada for a causeway and bridge across the marshes and Holland River to connect their settlements with those on Yonge Street. The government granted some funds and Robert Armstrong and his sons built the first corduroy road across the marsh and river as far as Churchill to the north. From 1833 there was a daily stage coach service from York to Holland Landing and back. People, mail, and freight continued their way by water on the steamboat Colborne which passed around the lake twice a week or by means of the Holland River. In 1850, the Beaver and the Morning were added to the steamboat service, and the stagecoach line was extended to Bradford to meet the Beaver at the bridge. Excursion parties were run and the number of boats increased, so popular was the service on the lake. Stage and boat service predated the railway, but by the middle of the century, railway excitement ran high and aroused considerable controversy. Fearing increased taxation, the owners of lots in the Old Survey (Yonge Street south of the river and Holland Landing) seceded from Simcoe and the present boundary between York and Simcoe Counties was established.

Bradford United Church Situated on Barrie Street, or Highway 11/Yonge Street, the church was formerly the Methodist Church of Bradford and dates back to 1836. When Wesleyan Methodists of Bradford acquired the deed of the present property, they built the brick church which still stands in use and dedicated it in 1865. The circuit then included Bradford, Bond Head, Penville, Newton Robinson, Sutherland's, Ebenezer, and Mount Pleasant. The first musical instrument was a hand organ. The next, a reed organ, was replaced in 1870 by a pipe organ and in 1897 by the present pipe organ.

This farmhouse, more than 135 years old, was the home of the tollgate keeper on the Old Amsterdam Toll Road.

The Lukes House 1876-1994 On the west side of Barrie/Yonge Street, this Victorian villa with its balconied campanile was built for lawyer, John McLean Stevenson, who was Reeve from 1871 to 1877. Many prominent Bradford residents lived here. From 1910 until 1949 it was the home of the family of Samuel Lukes who owned the local flour mill.

The Bradford Post Office opened in 1835 with J. Peacock as the first postmaster. The postmaster in 1875 was H. S. Broughton who was followed by William Wood in 1916. He hired Broughton's daughter to take charge. When Wood died, the appointment fell to George D. Morton who kept Miss Broughton on until her retirement in 1941.

Men and horses were conveyed on scows to cut hay in the Holland marshes.

The Otonabee at Bradford around 1900.

INNISFIL

THE TOWNSHIP OF INNISFIL THE POETIC NAME FOR IRELAND

Innisfil was surveyed in 1820. It has a total area of 68,653 acres. After the survey, the first settlers were the Hewson family, who came by way of the Holland River and Lake Simcoe to settle at what they called Hewson's Point, later named Big Bay Point. David and James Soules came soon after, and were followed by the Clement, Lewis, Perry and Warnica families.

The first sawmill in the township was built at what is now called Tollendal by George McMullen in 1823. At the time the road was put through, a town was laid out at this point where the bay intersected the road on its straight path to the north.

Twelve years after the McMullen sawmill, the first grist mill was built, this being a mill to grind wheat into flour, and the customer usually paid for the grinding by leaving a portion of the wheat called a "grist" with the miller.

A settlement was growing in the corner of the township, and Mr. Francis Hewson was appointed magistrate. He became the first legal representative of the township, and performed marriages and administered justice. The first white child born in the township was Anna Hewson.

In 1821, Jacob Gill located on Lot 23 Concession 2, where he was the sole disturber of the woodland peace for a number of years. During the next ten years came the Allans, Climies, Boyes, DeNures, Hattons, Jacks, Lauries, Longs, McConchies, Maneers, McConkeys, McCulloughs, McLeans, Rogersons, Thomsons, Todds, Wallaces, Wrights, Duncans, Reives, Barclays, and the Cross family. Still other were to come.

In the next four years, post offices, churches, and stores were established, also a form of local government under commissioners appointed by a provincial act. The first post office, then called Innisfil, was on Lot 15 Concession 8; it was later known as the Barclay Post Office and is now called Barclay's Corners.

The first school is said to have been at Victoria (now Stroud), and the first teacher a Mr. Booth. The first church was also at Stroud, and was Methodist. Before this, services had been held in various homes. The first regular Christian missionary was James Currie.

Every side-line in Ontario is rich in memories of the joys and sorrows of the pioneers. In some of them may be gathered stories of tragedies rivalling in interest anything told of the lands of chivalry and romance.

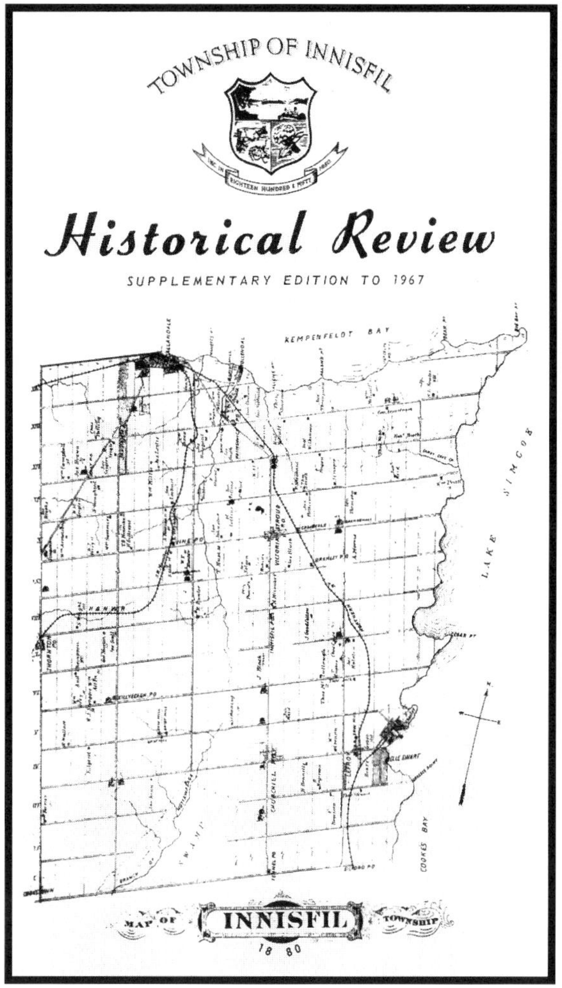

Cherry Creek School is one of the oldest schools in the Township of Innisfil. The first building was log, the second frame, and the present 1876 building is of brick. At one time, 100 pupils attended, taking their stone ink bottles across the road to Mr. Mains where the storekeeper ladled out homemade ink for a penny.

PIONEER ROAD BUILDERS

George Frederick Hanning Warnica, a Dane, settled in Salina, New York, and married Catherine Myers, a German woman. They had four sons: John, George Frederick, William, and Joseph. After the War of 1812-15, attracted by the offer of free grant lands made by the Canadian government, they moved to Markham Township in 1815. In 1823, the Warnica family moved into the bush in Innisfil some miles west of Big Bay Point. They cleared a patch of ground and built a small log house where the village of Painswick now is. Shortly after, the family harvested their first crop of wheat despite warnings that the hordes of blackbirds would surely destroy it.

About the time of their arrival in Innisfil a movement was on foot among the settlers of the Penetanguishene district to have the "Main Road" opened through Innisfil and thus complete overland communication between Lakes Huron and Ontario. All parts of the highway except through Innisfil, by this time, had been constructed. To do this, a sufficient sum of money was raised by subscription. The two eldest sons, John and George, secured the contract for the construction of this road from the head of Kempenfeldt Bay as far south as the present site of Churchill, a distance of eleven miles. This work was performed in the autumn of the same year in which they came to

Innisfil, viz, 1825, and for it they received the sum of $55, being the rate of $5 per mile. The contract for the remaining part from Churchill to West Gwillimbury was secured by John Cayton of the latter place. He, however, had little acquaintance with the forest, and was obliged to employ the brothers, John and George, to open his portion of the road also. This forest track which they were first to open throughout the entire length of Innisfil was rough and winding at first, but it was straightened in subsequent years.

SOCIAL HISTORY

FARMS

Much of Yonge Street's traffic came from the farms of the area which produced goods for both the domestic market and for export. Lumber and building materials, fresh fruit and vegetables, milk, eggs, meats, fish from the commercial fisheries, feed for livestock, wool and woven materials like homespun or skeins of wool, plus firewood, were all headed for the domestic market. For export, there were furs, pot and pearl ashes, flour, grains including peas and beans, seeds, malt, beeswax, hemp, cut stone, hides and skins, staves and shingles, cheese, maple sugar, butter, some meats, and huge amounts of timber. Return traffic brought mail, manufactured goods, passengers, tradesmen, newspapers and magazines, books, tools, table and glassware. A measure of the amount of production may be taken in examining the tonnage that left Toronto harbour, and the amounts are astounding when measured against the size of the population.

Within what is now the heart of the Metropolitan area, there were working farms well into this century. The huge Baldwin estate, mostly forest and farmland, was not broken up until the 1870s. The young man with the box camera stands at a farm for sale on the northwest corner of Yonge and Eglinton in 1905. Notice that the telephone has been introduced, that there is a barn and a split-rail fence in the background.

The first market to be established was the Fish Market, shown here. Gradually, it migrated westwards and became the St Lawrence Market. The wedge-shaped Coffin building in the background was replaced by the present Gooderham building. The wharf in the background extends Yonge Street's reach.

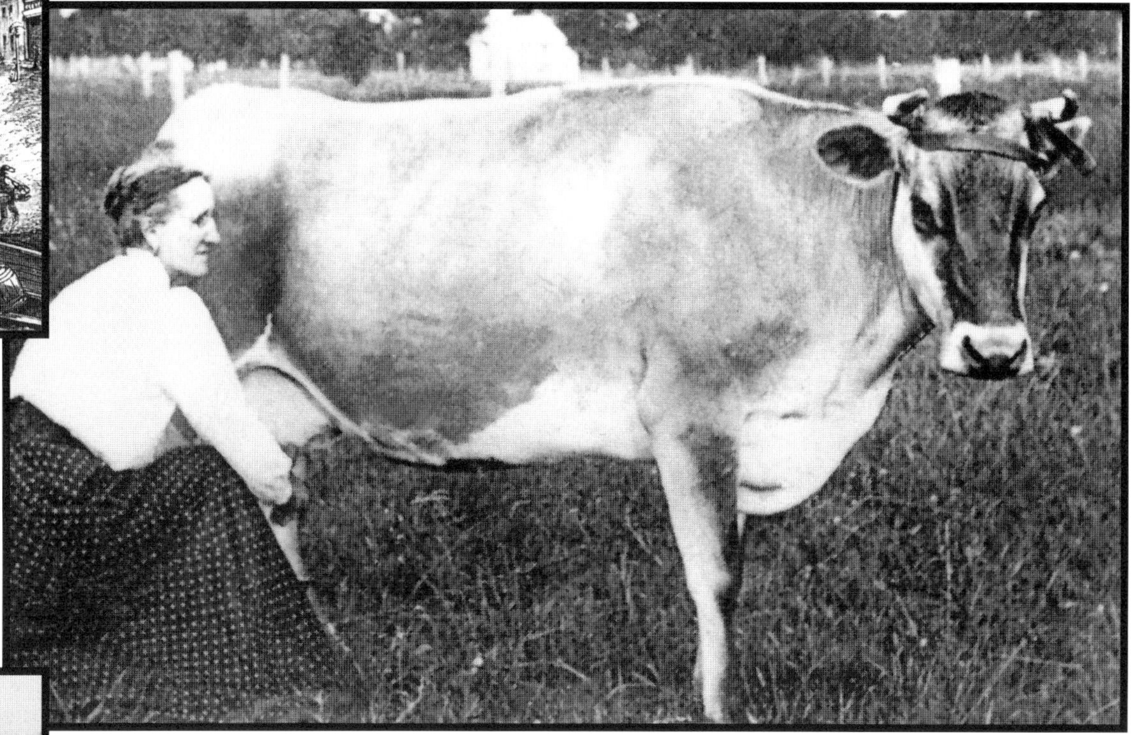

In 1909, the family's Jersey cow is being milked in the field at Yonge and Eglinton. The farmers of the region took their produce for sale to a variety of locations, the oldest and largest market being the famous St Lawrence Market. But there was a market behind the Yorkville Town Hall, and St Patrick's and St Andrew's Markets were west of Yonge downtown. Grain producers also sold large quantities to the breweries and distilleries which were numerous in the region.

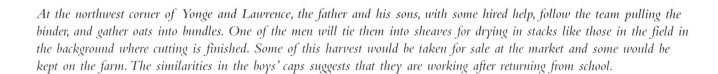

At the northwest corner of Yonge and Lawrence, the father and his sons, with some hired help, follow the team pulling the binder, and gather oats into bundles. One of the men will tie them into sheaves for drying in stacks like those in the field in the background where cutting is finished. Some of this harvest would be taken for sale at the market and some would be kept on the farm. The similarities in the boys' caps suggests that they are working after returning from school.

NATURAL HERITAGE

White Pine: official tree of Ontario; some still grow on valley and ravine edges, though these are badly affected by air pollution.

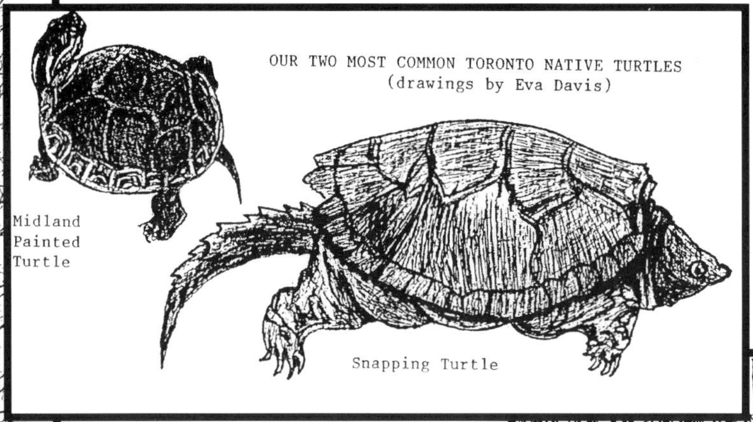

Turtles: several species can still be found in this region.

Toronto's once vast forests of White Pine and Oaks have been reduced to remnants in our parklands.

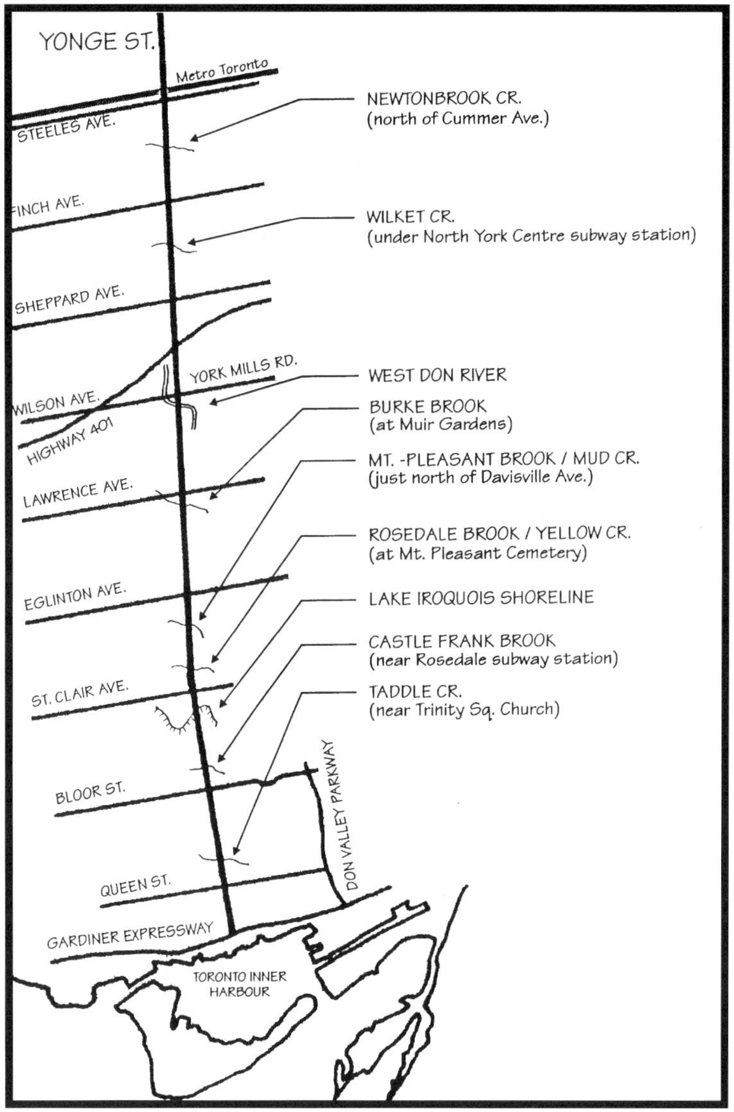

Creeks, rivers and landforms crossed by Yonge St. between Lake Ontario and Steeles Ave.

Only the West Don River still runs above ground. The rest crossed by Yonge Street are buried, though clues to their existence, such as dips in the road and nearby parks, can still be found on the landscape.

Where Toronto's creeks run through deep ravines, a system of linear parks contains remnants of the region's natural heritage of plants and animals.

Frogs: several species are still found in Toronto, but the filling-in of wet areas in valleys and ravines has reduced their numbers

INNS, HOTELS & TAVERNS

An astounding number of inns, hotels, and taverns operated on Yonge Street in the nineteenth century.

From the American Hotel at Front Street to the Green Bush Inn at Steeles Avenue, travellers had many opportunities to stop for refreshments. In the countryside north of Bloor there was a tavern about every half mile.

In the early days accommodation was not often up to Old World standards. One unhappy traveller described conditions in 1820 as follows:

"At inferior boarding-houses the accommodations are not comfortable or convenient or good. The company consists of all classes, from the man of independent property to the mechanic. The beds are indifferent, and from four to ten are crowded in one room, destitute of curtains, etc., and swarming with fleas and bugs. In such houses there is no such thing as comfort or privacy. Inns of the second class bear a great resemblance to the latter kind of boarding-houses."

Top: The furniture of a bar-room, excepting its characteristic accompaniments, consists of nothing more than a plain cherry table, two or three pine benches, and a fire-poker. It has also "whitewashed wall" and "nicely sanded floor". The bar-room of the Red Lion pictured above matches the description of an early traveller.
Above: Anderson's Hotel, Store, Hogg's Hollow, pre-1828 to 1856.

Top: The Red Lion was conveniently located just north of the toll gate on Yonge Street near Bloor. Farmers on their way to market could avoid paying the toll twice by staying the night and making an early start into the city in the morning.

Above: The ballroom of the Red Lion, described in John Ross Robertson's Landmarks of Toronto, as 40 x 20 feet and 18 feet high with an arched ceiling.

Inns played an important role in the social and political life of Upper Canadians. The local inn often served as an informal community centre where neighbours could meet and exchange information. Inns also played an official role in forming political opinion. The ballroom of a country inn might be designated as the township meeting hall and, on occasion, polling stations were set up in a public room at an inn.

The Yonge Street inns featured here played significant roles in the Rebellion of 1837 as meeting places for rebels.

In a remarkable show of support, William Lyon Mackenzie was re-elected at the polling station in the Red Lion Inn on January 2nd 1832 after being expelled from the Legislature on December 12, 1831.

Mackenzie, shown at the right, was also Toronto's first Mayor in 1834, the year of incorporation, and grandfather of William Lyon Mackenzie King, Prime Minister of Canada.

The American Hotel stood at the southwest corner of Yonge and Front from 1840 to 1889. Visible from the harbour, it was one of the better hotels in this highly competitive district.

The Bird in the Hand was John Montgomery's first tavern, built about 1820 north of modern Finch Avenue. When Montgomery moved to new premises on Yonge Street just north of Eglinton Avenue, John Finch rented this northern property and changed the name to Finch's Tavern.

The reputation of a hotel was often closely-linked to the landlord, and landlords changed locations frequently. John Montgomery was outstanding for his political activism as well as for the many inns he opened and operated.

When John Montgomery was sentenced to hang for his involvement in the Rebellion of 1837 he is reported to have said, "You think you can send me to the gallows, but I tell you that when you're all frizzling with the devil, I'll be keeping tavern on Yonge street."

After his pardon in 1845, John Montgomery did indeed return to keep a tavern on Yonge Street.

The original Green Bush Inn stood on the northeast corner of Steeles Avenue and Yonge Street. When the 1830 building was destroyed by fire, Joseph Abrahams moved to Queen Street and opened another inn of the same name.

The establishment most recently known as the Jolly Miller began as the second York Mills Hotel. The first hotel in this location was destroyed by fire around 1856. The stable and sheds were saved by a community bucket brigade passing buckets of water hand to hand from the mill pond to the buildings.

The Sun Tavern was built at the northwest corner of Yonge and Queen by John McIntosh in 1825. A Reform party meeting place, William Lyon Mackenzie once addressed a crowd of supporters gathered on the street from an upper storey window.

John Montgomery's Tavern, as it is known now, was named the Sickle and Sheath, a gathering place for Reformers. It was here that Colonel Moodie (pictured right) met his end, and Mackenzie's supporters made their last stand (pictured above) in the Rebellion of 1837.

The Golden Lion was established by Thomas Sheppard in 1825 on Yonge Street near modern Sheppard Avenue. The life-size carved and gilded lion that served as the sign over the door survives today in the bar of the Novotel Hotel. The lion is not visible in the photograph above, but is clearly pictured in the drawing above to the right.

PARADES

Apart from being a settlement road, a route connected to the military defence of the capital city, Yonge Street has been a parade route. The first major parade was the march of the farmers down most of the length of Yonge Street on December 5, 1837 to make clear the need for reform of government. Col. Moodie, an officer commanding government forces, was killed at Montgomery's Inn, north of Eglinton, during that march and two of the rebels, lieutenants of William Lyon Mackenzie, were captured and put to death for their part in that famous rebellion. Years later, farmers marched again to try to get the government to pave Yonge Street. Military units paraded on Yonge forever afterwards, on the way to fight the Riel Rebellion, on the way to the Boer War, to World Wars I and II. Veterans march to the cenotaph in front of the Old City Hall to remember those who fell during those wars. And there were many victory parades down Yonge at war's end. There have been parades for almost every reason: St Patricks Day; the "Glorious Twelfth"; winning the Grey or Stanley Cup in sport; Labour Day; and, once, when a section of Yonge Street was painted pink for the occasion, the great ballet dancer, Rudolph Nureyev, danced up Yonge Street.

EATON'S DAILY STORE NEWS

HURRAH! SANTA CLAUS COMES SATURDAY MORNING

Toyland in New Store North-west Cor. James and Albert

With Band Playing, Banners Gaily Waving, Prancing White Horses, a Gorgeous Gold Car, Santa Claus, with great pomp, makes his formal glorious entrance to his new home, North-West Cor. Albert and James Sts., across from Store.

LEAVING YORK MILLS AT ABOUT 8.30 A.M. AND TRAVELING SLOWLY DOWN YONGE STREET. Santa Claus comes with a bodyguard mounted on beautiful white, prancing horses, and a gorgeous car of gold with a throne made of four huge candy canes and a gold canopy; he has his very own band in uniform, and a real, live Gnome. Santa Claus will have the greatest cavalcade that has ever come to Toyland. A special bodyguard will meet him at Albert and Yonge streets and conduct him to the Second Floor of his great, new home, where there is a magnificent ice workshop with a fireplace, down which Santa comes. He has here a real Punch and Judy Show, also a Family of "Toyland Talking Tots"—funny figures that talk, and laugh, and sing. And with him is a wonderful little Gnome, who helps him in his undertakings and accompanies him on his travels. All this takes place in a gorgeous scene from the far North. There are Icebergs, a great, mysterious cave, and sparkling and beautiful Aurora Borealis. Santa will appear on the stage immediately upon his arrival, and everybody is requested to keep moving along, so that everybody will get an opportunity to see. On the Main Floor there's a great jungle scene—wild tigers, and bears, and lions, and a tree of chattering monkeys, as well as ferocious leopards and elephants. And there's the grand waterfall

Perhaps the most famous of the annual parades was begun in 1905 and ran for several years from York Mills south to Eaton's store at Queen Street, including, as the advertisement above announces, 1912. The parade, created by the T. Eaton Company, was the Santa Claus Parade, and its destination in the Eaton Store was a magical place called Toyland. For royal visits in the 19th century, huge triumphal arches covered with fresh greenery were built. Cross streets were usually involved as well, as the picture on the left shows; here, the city celebrates the Diamond Jubilee of Queen Victoria in 1897 and King Street's buildings are highly decorated in keeping with the festive decorations placed on Yonge by the Eaton's and Simpson's stores. Celebrating on Yonge Street is a tradition nearly 200 years old.

THEATRES

From the earliest years, York/Toronto had a cultural life, beginning with the lectures and recitals at the Mechanics' Institute, through various types of costumed entertainments and theatricals. Albert Hall, shown here, was built at 191 Yonge near Queen in 1874, and was used for chamber music, opera, and balls. The hall, like many of the time, was on the second floor, while the street level had commercial tenants. The original of this view of 1877 is in the City of Toronto Archives.

The old Toronto Opera House on Yonge, north of King, was destroyed by fire in 1903, but by fall of that year the new Majestic Music Hall had been built on the site, although this name was not used for it until 1910. The halls had been managed by Ambrose Small and, when the theatre magnate mysteriously disappeared in 1919, the building was sold to J.P. Bickell, first president of Maple Leaf Gardens. He and his partners renovated and converted it into a movie theatre named the Regent. In 1920, Bickell's group and another formed Famous Players Canadian Corporation and celebrated with a film starring Mary Pickford.

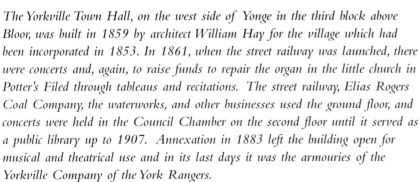

On Shuter Street, half a block from Yonge, is the grand old lady of concert halls, Massey Hall, so named because it was built with a donation by Hart Massey. Almost every major performing arts group played on its stage, from the Birdsall School of Dance and the Volkoff Ballet Company to youth orchestras. It was the home, for many years, of the Toronto Symphony and the Mendelssohn Choir. Acoustically, it has no equal in Toronto's history. With the opening of the new concert hall on King Street, Massey Hall is used today for a variety of concerts.

The Yorkville Town Hall, on the west side of Yonge in the third block above Bloor, was built in 1859 by architect William Hay for the village which had been incorporated in 1853. In 1861, when the street railway was launched, there were concerts and, again, to raise funds to repair the organ in the little church in Potter's Filed through tableaus and recitations. The street railway, Elias Rogers Coal Company, the waterworks, and other businesses used the ground floor, and concerts were held in the Council Chamber on the second floor until it served as a public library up to 1907. Annexation in 1883 left the building open for musical and theatrical use and in its last days it was the armouries of the Yorkville Company of the York Rangers.

From the time the Auditorium was completed in 1931 in the new Eaton's College Street Store, the hall was a showplace and the toast of the city for both its beauty and acoustics. Chamber music, soloists from around the world, opera concerts by the Royal Conservatory's Opera School, marionettes, and travelogues were all presented. The last concert was given in 1977, and the future of the great auditorium is undecided.

Places of Worship

SHORELINE TO HOLLAND LANDING

Holy Blossom Congregation

The first location for the Holy Blossom congregation was the Albert Ascher house, and the second location is marked by a plaque at the southeast corner of Yonge and Richmond Streets. The third location was a red brick building designed by Stewart and Strickland on Richmond Street east of Victoria from 1876 to 1897. Another congregation, formed in 1849, began to meet in the Richmond and Yonge Location, on the third floor over Coombes Drugstore. The Holy Blossom congregation went on to a fourth location, shown above, a Moorish style building designed by Sidall at 115 Bond Street on the east side between Dundas and Gould. This building was sold in 1938 to St George's Greek Orthodox Church and the Holy Blossom congregation moved to its present location, the magnificent synagogue on Bathurst Street.

Davenport Road Methodist/Mission

The Davenport and Yonge Street Primitive Methodist congregation had been meeting in a modest frame building from 1844 to 1866 on the south side of Sydenham Street (now Cumberland) in Yorkville. In 1866, they erected this building, seating 250 people, on the northwest corner of Davenport Road and Yonge Street on land donated by Robert Walker. In 1886, after the union of the various Methodist bodies, it was found that the Yonge Street church was not large enough and a new site was purchased on the southeast corner of Avenue Road and Webster Avenue. A larger building, seating 900, was erected there and named St Paul's Methodist. The old church was rented in 1891 for two years, free of charge, to the Anglican Davenport Road Mission, a mission of the Church of the Redeemer who had been meeting at 147 Davenport Road, and, when they moved, they became known as the Church of the Messiah. Next, the old building was sold to the Christian Workers who, under P.W. Philpott, formerly connected with the Salvation Army, had an active congregation of fifty to sixty members. The lovely building was demolished in 1910 to make way for the present Masonic Temple.

Yorkminster-Park Baptist Church

When Bloor Street Baptist Church required new facilities, a fine Gothic limestone building was erected in 1928 on Yonge Street on the northeast corner of Heath. It was named Yorkminster Baptist Church. In 1961, a fire demolished Park Road Baptist Church, and the two congregations joined to form Yorkminster-Park Baptist Church in the Yorkminster building at 1585 Yonge. A Chinese Baptist congregation shares the north building on the site.

Davisville Methodist

"Pottery Corner" was the early location of Davisville Methodist Church. As early as 1851, the congregation met in a frame building, later constructing a fine, brick church and then bricked over the original building for a Sunday School. The new building had a slate roof with polychrome detailing in it, and there was an attractive little bellcote. In 1925, this congregation became Glebe Road United and the former building at 1992 Yonge was occupied by Hope Gospel. In 1970, the building was sold as a store.

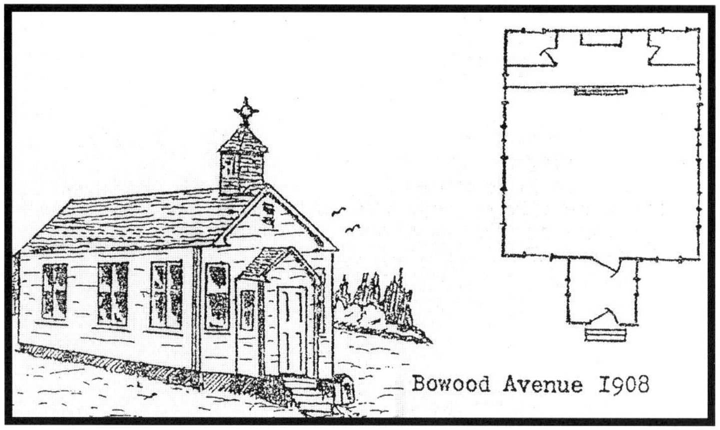

St. Leonard's Anglican

The congregation met first in a simple frame building on Bowood Avenue between Yonge and Bowcastle in 1908. The present brick building was built in 1921 and was a mission of St. Clement's (Eglinton).

Eglinton Wesleyan Methodist/United

In 1830, their first location was a log schoolhouse on the west side of Yonge Street. Then the congregation met on Glengrove Avenue, and next on the east side of Yonge Street in 1834. In 1925, the present brick building was constructed. The premises are shared with Finnish A Teras and Korean congregations.

Fairlawn Methodist/United

Also known as Bedford Park Methodist, the congregation met in the Bedford Hotel on Yonge Street at Fairlawn from 1914 to 1920. Then the members built a frame building on the east side of the present lot. In 1924, a brick building was constructed adjacent to the old building. In 1989, the congregation amalgamated with Armour Heights to become Fairlawn Heights United.

Blessed Sacrament

People interested in forming a Roman Catholic congregation met in private homes before the formal organization of the church in 1926. The present building, designed by J. Gibb Morton, is Gothic in design and was completed June 30, 1930.

St. John's Anglican (York Mills)

In 1797, parishioners met in Seneca Ketchum's home on Yonge Street. In 1812, they met in an old log schoolhouse on Old Yonge Street. In 1816, the parish was established. In 1843, a yellow brick Gothic style church, designed by John George Howard, was built on Lot 11, Conc 1E, on land donated by Joseph Sheppard. The address today is 19 Don Ridge Drive, but the church building by Howard has not moved. St. John's York Mills was the first outpost of St. James' Anglican in Toronto.

York Mills Presbyterian

The congregation formed in 1836 and met in a building on the east side of Yonge near Ivor Road (Lot 10, Conc 1E); this building was subsequently torn down. In 1859, the congregation rebuilt on Lot 10, Conc 1W with the same material. This building too was demolished. The third location was at the corner of Leslie and Lawrence Avenue in 1885, and this building was purchased by Bethesda Primitive Methodists. In 1890, they joined Bethesda Presbyterian.

Evangel Temple

Members of this congregation first met in the historic Bond Street Congregational building on the northeast corner of Dundas and Bond Streets in Toronto. This building is the one pictured above, and was designed by E. J. Lennox. It was purchased from the Congregationalists by the Pentecostal Assemblies of Canada and was renamed "Evangel Temple". A disastrous fire in September 1981 destroyed the magnificent building of Georgetown stone. The congregation built a modern brick building on land they owned on Yonge Street just south of Highway 401, on the northwest corner of Carson Crescent.

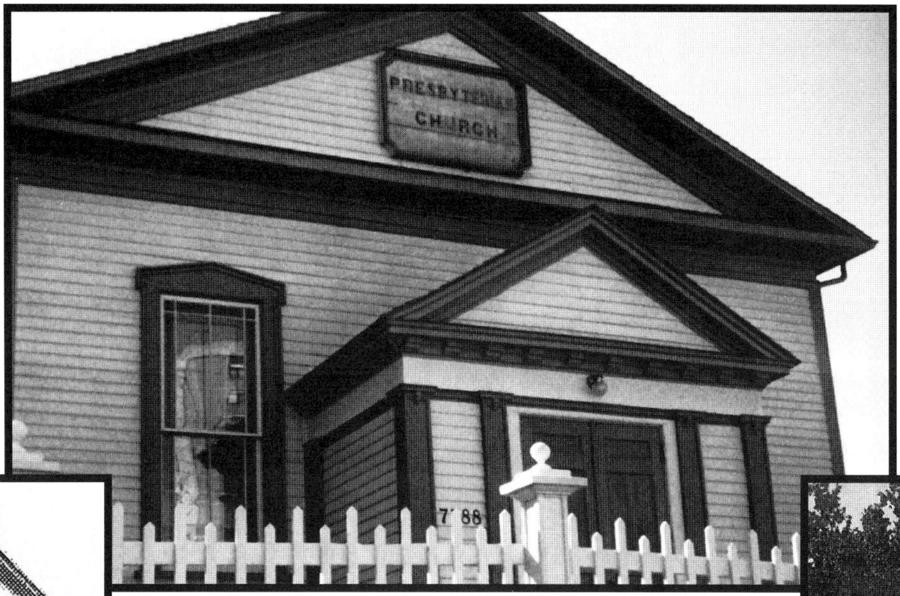

British Wesleyan Methodist Church (Thornhill)

A building erected on Centre Street a few steps from Yonge was purchased by Presbyterians in 1850 and moved to its present site on Yonge north of Centre Street.

St. Edward The Confessor (Lansing)

Known earlier as St. Edward's Roman Catholic Church Mission, the congregation met first in the home of Raymond Riddell on Sheppard Avenue. In 1923, they met on Spring Garden Avenue in a building seating 125. In 1952, a brick building, designed by J. Hoffa, was built at 4935 Yonge Street. Before 1842, the congregation was a mission of St. Mary Immaculate.

Lansing Methodist/United

In 1918, members met on Spring Garden Avenue. Rev T.W. Picket purchased the Golden Lion Hotel on the west side of Yonge south of Sheppard Avenue (shown above) and built a portable unit. Land for the present building was purchased in 1941 and, in 1951, a modern building designed by Craig and Madill, was erected. From 1925 to 1938, joint services were held with Willowdale Methodists and Zion Primitive Methodists.

Willowdale Methodist/United

The congregation met first in 1796. In 1816, a log building was erected on Lot 19, Conc 1E, on the northeast corner of Yonge and Church Streets. Jacob Cummer donated land in 1834 and, in 1836, a yellow brick building was constructed, then sold to the Seventh Day Adventists. The church was also known as Cummer's Chapel and Willowdale Meeting House. It became Willowdale United in 1925, and shared premises with Hanmin Logos congregation in 1996.

Vishnu Mandir (Richmond Hill)

On the west side of Yonge Street north of Highway 7 at 8640 Yonge is the largest Hindu Temple in the region. It contains a library as well. The sculpture close to the street is of Mahatma Gandhi, beloved by the world.

The Anglican Church of St. Mary (Richmond Hill)

The little yellow brick church known as St. Mary's was dedicated in 1872 by Bishop A. N. Bethune. The land was donated by John Robert Arnold, U.E.L., whose family burying ground is surrounded by the church complex.

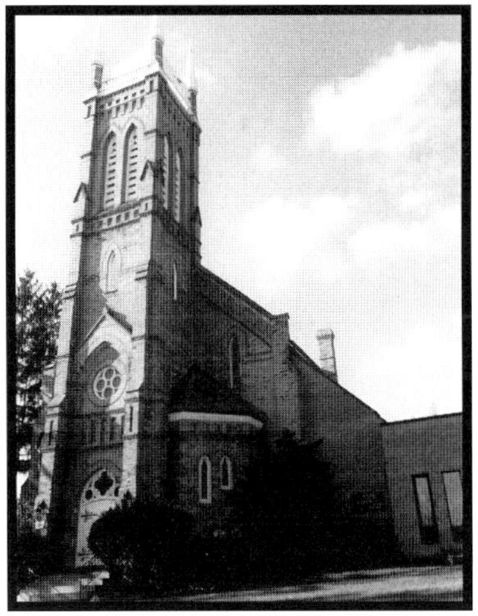

Richmond Hill Presbyterian

The Presbyterians in Richmond Hill first met in 1817 in a log schoolhouse on the James Miles farm, part of Lot 46, Conc 1, of Vaughan. In 1821, James Miles donated the land, and a frame building was erected. This building was sold in 1881 and used as a barn. In 1880, the yellow brick building designed by Langley, Langley and Burke was erected on the west side of Yonge Street north of Major Mackenzie Drive at 10066 Yonge Street.

Richmond Hill Wesleyan Methodist/United

A log cabin served this Methodist congregation from 1810 until 1847, when a frame church was built on a half-acre site, across Centre Street from the present church. The church burned to the ground in 1879, and was replaced by the present building on land donated by Abraham Law in 1880.

St. Mary Immaculate Roman Catholic (Richmond Hill)

Located on two acres of land on Mill Street, the original frame building was dedicated on September 20, 1857. A new brick church was erected in 1896, and it was replaced in 1968 by the present structure at 10259 Yonge on the northeast corner. It was paid for by the late Stephen Roman.

St. John's Anglican (Jefferson)

This congregation was established in 1848. The church was erected in 1849-1850 on the west part of Lot 60, Conc 1E – land which had been donated by Captain Martin MacLeod of Drynoch. The church was consecrated by Bishop John Strachan in 1856 as the Church of St. John the Martyr.

St. Andrew's College Chapel

Originally, St. Andrew's College was in Rosedale, Toronto. A new chapel was built in 1926 when the College moved to the west side of Yonge Street in Aurora. Donated by Joseph Flavelle, the chapel was built in memory of the 106 students lost in World War I. Its Georgian style was designed by Marani and Paisley.

Hicksite Meeting House (Armitage)

Certain members of the Religious Society of Friends separated from the Orthodox Friends and erected a white frame building on the west side of Yonge, south of Mulock Drive in Newmarket in 1829. It was demolished in 1940. A plaque marks the site and the adjoining cemetery.

Upper Yonge Cemeteries

NORTH TORONTO TO HOLLAND LANDING

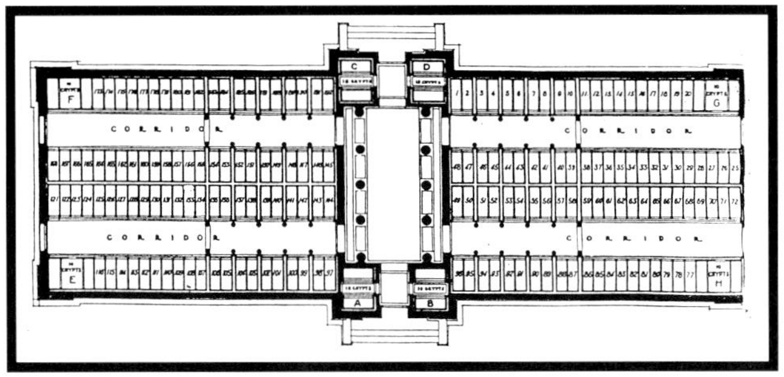

Forest Lawn Mausoleum Cemetery

Built of concrete block, the two original massive buildings have interiors of Italian white marble, spacious foyers with vaulted ceiling and beautiful stained glass windows. Long corridors are lined with crypts, each containing five compartments. Private rooms are entered through grilled doorways. Following a full military service in St. James' Cathedral, Sir Henry Pellatt, builder of Casa Loma, was laid to rest in one of these.

Cummer Burial Grounds

In 1834, the estate of Abraham Johnson donated one-half acre of land for a cemetery, to adjoin "Cummer's Chapel". When Yonge Street was widened, some of the grave markers were moved to a cairn, and the graveyard was enclosed by a fence. The two stones shown at left are the markers for the graves of Abraham Johnson and Jacob Cummer.

Holy Trinity Anglican Cemetery

Located on the west side of Yonge Street, this churchyard cemetery originally encompassed three acres and is surrounded by a wrought-iron fence. Worthy of note is the burial here of Colonel Robert Moodie, shot by rebels at Montgomery's Tavern on the first night of the 1837 Rebellion. Outbreaks of contagious diseases – cholera in 1832 and diphtheria in 1874 – are reflected on these early tombstones.

Friends' Hicksite Burying Ground (Armitage)

Only the cemetery remains in the churchyard on the west side of Yonge Street. The early Quakers did not permit the use of grave markers and were buried in order of death. Later, when permitted, grave markers were of fieldstone, wood or marble.

Trinity Anglican Church Cemetery, (Aurora)

According to the Church's Centennial History of 1946, a new church was built in 1883-4. The old church was demolished and the graves surrounding the old church were removed to the Aurora Cemetery. "The records of the parish were deposited in a tin box in the northeast corner of the new church in the second course of bricks." The new church was opened March 14, 1884. There are nine remaining markers at the back of the present church, close to the wall.

St. John's Anglican Church Cemetery (Jefferson)

St. John's Anglican Church Cemetery is located on the west part of Lot 60, Conc 1E, Township of Markham, the site of the de Puisaye Settlement of 1799.

Christ Church Cemetery (Holland Landing)

The land for the cemetery was a part of Town Lot 107, Conc 1E, of Yonge, and had been owned by Peter Robinson. Two years after his death in 1838, the lot was extended eastward and a similar plot was laid out west of Yonge Street. The southwest corner was set aside for a cemetery and for an Anglican church which was built in 1843 and named Christ Church.

ST. MICHAEL'S CEMETERY

Many markers commemorate Toronto Catholics who died before the cemetery opened, like this one for Henry Hughes, who may have been moved from St. Paul's churchyard on Queen Street East.

St. Michael's Cemetery was opened in 1855 on the west side of Yonge Street, just south of St. Clair Avenue in an area called Deer Park. At that time it was a healthy distance from the city, but now the cemetery is almost hidden amidst the stores, office buildings and residences of mid-town Toronto.

St. Michael's was the second Roman Catholic cemetery in Toronto, replacing the churchyard of St. Paul's on Queen Street East.

An example of a "white bronze" marker from the 1880s. The components were cast of a metal alloy and then bolted together.

Many of the grave markers, like this one for Jane Flynn, now lie flat.

This modest hand-carved stone for Syrian pedlar Cannae Sheyeke, who died in 1900 of consumption, was photographed in 1991.

MOUNT PLEASANT CEMETERY

This Mausoleum commemorates Captain James Fluke, a sea captain who moved to Toronto from Blackstock and who lived on King Street near Spadina. His wife erected this monument. She remarried, and died 24 years later.

In 1873, 200 acres of land on the east side of Yonge Street, south of the Village of Davisville, were purchased for a non-denominational burying ground, to be named Mount Pleasant. It was opened to the public in 1875. More than 175,000 burials have been recorded. Mount Pleasant is the third cemetery established by the Toronto General Burying Grounds (which became the Toronto Trust Cemeteries). It contains some reburials in a special section reserved for pioneers. These bodies were removed from the oldest cemetery, Potter's Field, which was located at Yonge and Bloor. Today, the Trust (now Commemorative Services of Ontario) is responsible for nine cemeteries. Mount Pleasant serves, not only as a burial ground, but as a park with special horticultural features, a protected area for wildlife, and is a major heritage site for Toronto.

That Toronto is a city built by immigrants is readily apparent in a visit to Mount Pleasant, from the Irish, who came in the 1840s, to the most recent arrivals. This red granite monument shows the traditional Chinese Fu dogs.

A proper visit to Mount Pleasant Cemetery would take a day, as the grounds are extensive and the range of markers quite extraordinary. A goodly portion of Toronto's history rests in Mount Pleasant.

The most imposing structure in Mount Pleasant Cemetery is the mausoleum of the Massey family, built initially by Hart Massey for his two sons who had died earlier and, in whose memory, he also built Massey Hall and the Fred Victor Mission. A large number of family members are interred here.

POTTER'S FIELD CEMETERY

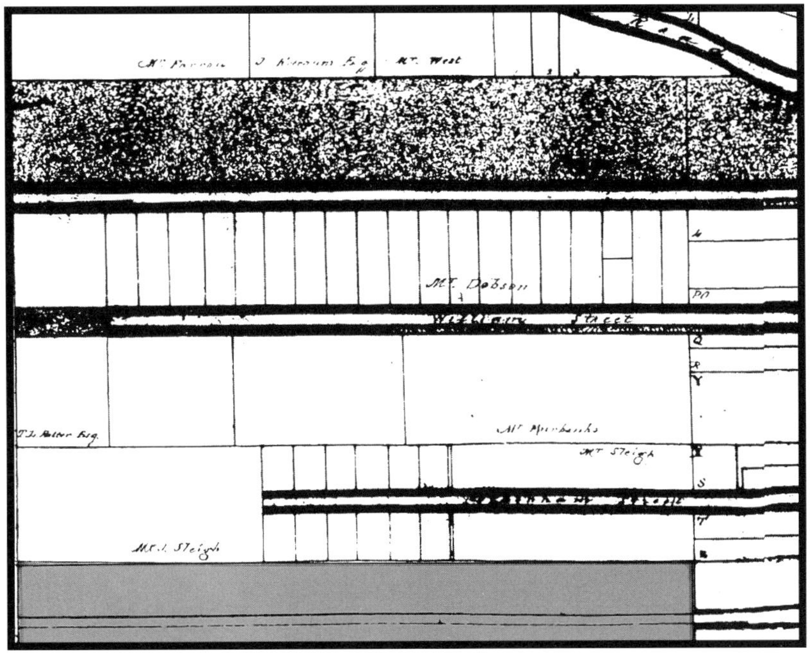

Until 1825, burials had been made along denominational lines and the need for a non-sectarian burial ground was recognized. In the same year, a meeting was held at the Masonic Hall in Yorkville, a Cemetery Trust was formed, property chosen, and a petition to the Legislature was drafted. Serving together on that committee were vehement political enemies – William Lyon Mackenzie and Thomas Carfrae. An Act was passed and the cemetery opened in 1826. The Liddy map above was drawn in 1853, the year Yorkville was incorporated, and it shows the laneway leading directly off Yonge westwards through the six-acre cemetery. The cemetery was along Bloor and south of Cumberland Street (then called Sydenham). The laneway there today, off both sides of Bay Street, marks the northern boundary of the cemetery.

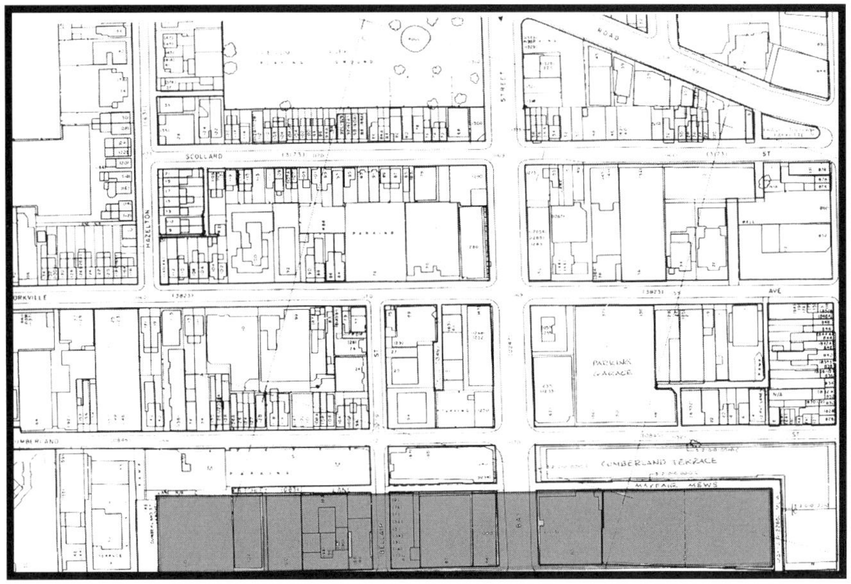

The shaded area on the city's 1985 Property Data Map shows the location of the cemetery. By the 1850s, Yorkville was growing and the cemetery was viewed as an obstacle to progress, and efforts began to close it. The last interment took place on 21 January 1855. In the thirty years it had been open, Potter's Field received 6,685 burials and the great effort of removing graves began.

The register of burials is a history book. There were cholera victims, many babies who died of problems that would be considered today as minor – such things as teething. The burial ground was used by Yorkvillers as a local cemetery and there were many residents buried there and, sometimes, a substantial number of family members. There were strangers about whom little was known, murders, suicides, victims of epidemics of all kinds. The number of small children buried there gives insight into medical practice of the times. Some very historic burials took place there: Samuel

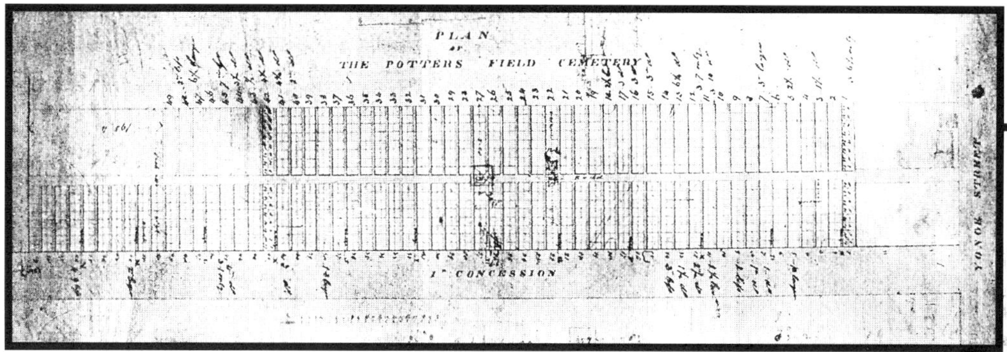

This plan of Potter's Field Cemetery was drawn in 1846 by John George Howard, a surveyor and architect of importance in Toronto's history. It shows clearly the position of the little church marking, half-way along the path which, by 1846, no longer led off Yonge Street. The Yonge frontages had always been commercial properties, but in the early years contained the house and grounds of the sexton. Above the northern boundary is what became the laneway that still runs eastward, as Mayfair Mews, and westward, as Critchley Lane, both city streets much more modest than Cumberland Street to the north.

The first burial in Potter's Field was that of the infant daughter of Thomas Carfrae, who died after a life of one day on 18 July 1826. The picture above is thought to have recorded that sad day. The church, or chapel in the cemetery, stood where Bay Street is today, and it had been the first St. Paul's Bloor Street [Anglican]. When that congregation began construction of the stone building known now as Cody Hall, the little wooden church was put on logs and rolled along Bloor Street into the position shown here. Over the years, it had various names, including St. Sepulchre, Church of the Redeemer (which it eventually became at yet another location), and St. Paul's Yorkville.

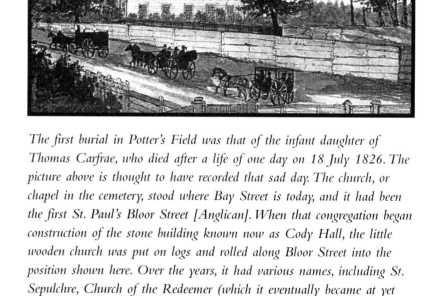

Lount and Peter Matthews are two of these. During the 1837 Rebellion, Lount and Matthews had been lieutenants of William Lyon Mackenzie. They were captured, tried for treason, hanged as traitors and buried in Potter's Field. When graves were moved after the cemetery closed, theirs were transferred to the Necropolis, but by this time, they were regarded as heroes, and a splendid monument marks their graves. Some of the causes of death are mysterious, such as "decline" or "inflammation" or "by a fall down a stair". From 1851 to 1881, there were 984 graves moved to the Necropolis, 364 to Mount Pleasant, and a few to other locations. Many were too deteriorated to move. Over 5000 graves are unaccounted for. When subdivision of the old cemetery lands began in the 1880s, houses were built over the remaining graves. When commercial buildings replaced the houses, the excavations removed most of the upper layers of the cemetery lands to landfill sites.

NEWSPAPERS

Many Upper Canadians subscribed to publications from the old world, from the United States, and from the older parts of Canada. But the need for information on local issues was always there, especially in the years leading up to the 1837 Rebellion. *The Upper Canada Gazette* or *American Oracle* had been established in 1793 and published as a semi-official recorder of government action. In 1820, John Carey founded *The Observer*, a weekly which was published into 1831. Opposite, *The Colonial Advocate*, was published from 1824 until 1834 when supporters of the government threw the owner's printing press into Toronto harbour. The publisher was William Lyon Mackenzie, a vociferous leader of rebel elements, who had rented his office from Robert Baldwin, whose quiet diplomacy and quiet behind-the-scenes work actually brought about Responsible Government. Before 1867 and Confederation, there were more than eighty newspapers and periodicals published in Toronto alone, in addition to broad-sheets posted in public places, and tracts given away or sold by those wishing to make a point. Mackenzie started a second newspaper in 1836, *The Constitution*, and *The Globe*, which later merged with *The Mail and Empire*, was begun in 1844. Among the newspapers was the *Provincial Freeman*, whose brilliant writer and editor was Mary Ann Shadd, the first woman and first black to publish a newspaper in Canada. In 1854, her office was half a block from Yonge Street but moved away from Toronto shortly afterwards.

Mary Ann Shadd

THE COLONIAL ADVOCATE.

[No. 131.]
[THIRD SERIES.]

YORK, THURSDAY. DECEMBER 6, 1827.

Office in King Street opposite the new Court House.
Printing House in Church Street, opposite the Canada Land Company's Office.

PRINTED AND PUBLISHED BY W. L. MACKENZIE, PRINTER TO THE HONOURABLE THE HOUSE OF ASSEMBLY OF UPPER CANADA.

...ts from the history of the destruction of the Colonial Advocate ...es, by officers of the provincial government of Upper Canada ... law students of the Attorney and Solicitor General, in open day ... in presence of the honourable William Allan, a police magistrate ... collector of the customs, and Stephen Heward Esquire, auditor ...eral of the colony.

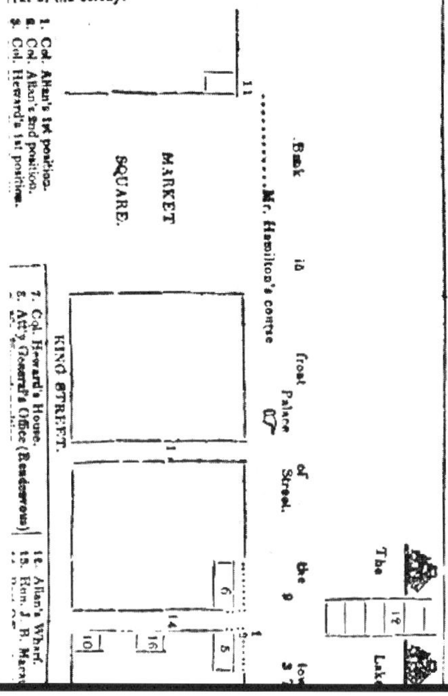

...confidence of the government.---Nine of the conspirators have been identified and sworn to---and in order to give the people a correct idea of the thing, it is necessary for us to state, that *five or six of the nine* are employed in the offices of the Governor, the Attorney General, and the Solicitor General--as clerks and law students!!!---What will the patriotic Doctor Lefferty say, at the next meeting of Parliament, when the Attorney General in the *loyal zeal* of the son of a U. E. Loyalist," exclaims that the Americans invaded our country---ransacked our towns---*destroyed our property---and murdered our wives and children*!"---We think we see the Doctor's indignant brow lowering upon him with the following appropriate retort---"Yes, Sir, the Americans invaded us and destroyed our property, as enemies, in open war---but *three emissaries*, as I am informed, from your office, and in your employment, *invaded the private abode of a fellow-subject and destroyed his property, in times of profound peace*---yet they afterwards remained in your employment, and enjoyed your confidence!"---What appears most extraordinary in this business is, that the official Gazette has been published a *second time* since the outrage was committed, without ever alluding to it---and to this circumstance, coupled with the situations of the conspirators, we wish particularly to direct the public attention.

[From the Upper Canada, Kingston Herald of June 20.]

PATRICIAN RIOT, AT YORK.

Such an annihilation of valuable property, such a daring breach of the peace, in the face of the government, such an insult upon the laws, such a conspiracy and outrage against the freedom of the Press, the palladium of civil rights, was never before witnessed, in this province, or any other Colony under the protection of British government and law. The riot was perpetrated with deliberation and manifest concert, with what the lawyers call "malice prepense." The perpetrators of it are said to be attached to, or connected with, and as it were selected and delegated from, almost all the public offices in York, from the Lieutenant Governor's office down to that of the Clerk of the Peace. It is also stated to have been committed in the presence of two Magistrates, who stood upon the bank, while the rioters, among whom was a son of one of them, were riotously carrying the types from the office to the bay, and these exemplary Conservators of the Peace, one of them a Legislative Councillor, and both of them loaded with public offices, witnessed the riot with apparent satisfaction, at least without any attempt to prevent the violation of law and destruction of property. It is so stated; but for the honour of the Government and the Province, we cannot but hope there is some mistake in the statement of so glaring and scandalous a fact.

The opponents of the Advocate, having the administration of the civil law in their own hands, had no occasion to resort to mob law. It is a pernicious precedent; an ill-advised and most dangerous experiment.—The stone, once "set a rolling," may roll back, and crush some of those who have thus rashly put it in motion. Mobocracy cannot be a desirable species of Government. Let mobs be rendered fashionable, by Governmental connivance or impunity, and no one can be sure that he will not be the next sacrifice. If this patrician Mob, for instance, planned and executed by officers, clerks and favourites of government, should be justified or excused for destroying a Press friendly to the rights of the people under the pretext, true or false, of provoking personalities published by the Editor, the People, in their turn, may learn to imitate the courtly example, and a plebian mob, excited by some offensive publication, may demolish the Government Press, or the office of one of the

BOARDERS WANTED.

THE subscriber can accomodate two young gentlemen with board and lodging; also stabling for two horses if required.

WILLIAM PHAIR.

King-Street Nov. 22nd.

NEW GUIDE TO HEALTH.

THE public are respectfully informed, that Samuel Thomson's patent right theory of practice, or Botanic family Physician, containing a complete system of practice, upon a plan entirely new, with descriptions of the vegetables made use of, and directions for preparing and administering them to cure diseases, has just been published. Much has been said about this mode of curing diseases, that it has ill effects; thousands have made use of this Medicine, and to which they are ready to attest of its utility, and that it is perfectly harmless. The Medical Doctors have spoke loudly against making use of Steam to remove disease, but of late they have invented vapor Baths themselves. Steam is the one thing, and of course will have the same effect. These vegatables may be used in perfect safety and have a good effect to cure all disease that is curable by art. The medicine is obtained on every man's farm, or may be cultivated, and whoever has become acquainted with this theory of practice, do consider it of inestimable value. The books may be obtained at Daniel Perry's Ernest Town, with the vegetables pulverised and fit for use; also of Lesslie & Sons, York; P... r McDonell, Whitby, and Andrew Heron Junior, Niagara; and the book is for sale at P. McPhail's.

ROBERT WILLIAMS.

Niagara, August 30th. 117.

E. PECK & CO.

BOOKSELLERS, ROCHESTER,

HAVE just published, and offer for sale, by the thousand or less quantity, the *Christian Almanack for* 1828; reprinted from a copy prepared under the direction and published for the benefit of the American Tract Society. The Rochester edition has calender pages fitted to this meridian. The price has been reduced since last year, and merchants and others will be furnished on the most reasonable terms. Also *the Western Almanack for* 1828, containing, besides the usual astronomical calculations, a great variety of useful and interesting matter. This edition will be sold very low. Also, just received, the *German Almanack for* 1828, of the Philadelphia and Baltimore editions.—Also for sale, a great variety of School Books and Stationary, at wholesale and retail, at

VALUABLE PROPERTY IN ST. DAVIDS.

TO LET for three or four years, or to sell on reasonable terms,—that property in the thriving village of St. David's owned by the subscriber, and consisting of a large brick dwelling-house, two acres of land, with orchards, gardens, out-houses, a good tannery, &c. The house and premises are in the best order, will be let together, and possession given immediately—they form a fit residence for a private gentleman, are in a very desirable, healthy, and romantic part of the country, about 8 miles from the Falls, 2 from Queenston, and within one mile of Stamford cottage the summer retreat of his excellency General Maitland.—If not let as a private house, it would answer for a hotel or tavern stand. Apply to Mr. George Shaw or Messrs. R. Woodruff & Co. at St. Davids, or to the subscriber at Streetsville by Trafalgar.

May 18th—103 tf. TIMOTHY STREET.

AGENCY NOTICE.

THE subscriber offers himself as an agent, and trusts that his experience in merchandise in general, and strict attention to, and punctuality in business, will be sufficient inducements for his friends and acquaintance, to forward such orders as they may wish to have executed in this place to Wm. KENYON.

Rochester, N. Y. Nov. 10, 1827. 129—8.

WHEREAS a report has been circulated that a quantity of Leather was taken out of my tan-yard during my late illness, with a view of defrauding myself and others, by a man named Sparror Wellington, by occupation a tanner and currier, who was in my employment during the past season. I hereby declare my perfect belief, that he is innocent of the charge---that it is unfounded and has been raised by the tongues of some malicious and slanderous persons. During his residence with me for eight months, I at all times found him sober, upright and punctually honest.

A. ROBINET.

Toronto, November 17th, 1827. 129---8.

UPPER CANADA WOOLEN FACTORY.

CARDING, Spinning, Weaving, Fulling, Dyeing and Cloth Dressing.

WILLIAM TAYLOR having rented the Machinery, Works, and Distillery of Mr. John Scarlet on the Humber, for a term of years, solicits the support of the customers and friends of that establishment, and assures the public that his best en-

A Royal Perspective

During the two centuries of its existence, Yonge Street has had many royal links and associations. It has been travelled by our Kings and Queens, by their heirs, members of their families, and by their official representatives, the Governor-General of Canada and the Lieutenant-Governors of the province.

Yonge Street is intersected by many streets named after members of the Royal Family, or representatives of our monarchs: King Street for George III, Adelaide for Queen Adelaide and Consort of William IV, Richmond for the Duke of Richmond who was Governor General of British North America from 1818 to 1819 and is an ancestor of Diana, Princess of Wales, Queen Street for Queen Victoria, Albert for Victoria's husband Prince Albert and Consort of Queen Victoria.

LT. GEN. JOHN GRAVES SIMCOE
1752-1806
Founder of York
First Lieutenant-Governor
Province of Upper Canada

Yonge Street was laid out from 1793 to 1796 by the first royal Governor of Upper Canada, John Graves Simcoe. His regiment, the Queen's Rangers, did much of the work.

200 years later.

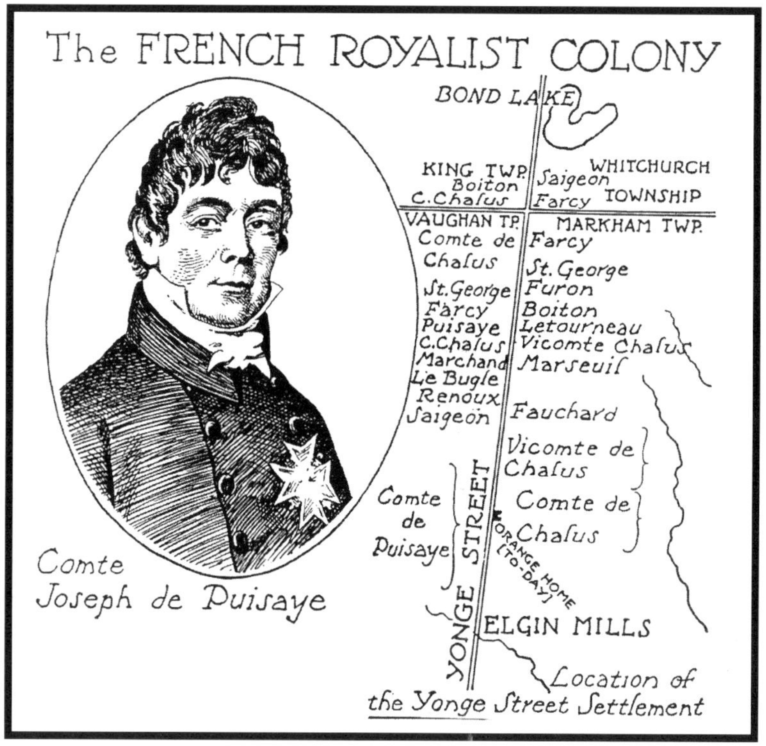

The Count de Puisaye, a French Royalist, attempted to found one of the earliest communities on Yonge Street in 1797.

King George and Queen Elizabeth, now Queen Mother, arrived in Toronto by train at the North Toronto Station on Yonge and Shaftesbury on May 22, 1939. The picture shows them as their car is about to proceed from the station onto Yonge. Their Toronto visit was a great event because they were the first of our reigning monarchs to tour Canada, and they came just as Canada was about to enter World War II.

Crowds of people camped out on Yonge Street in 1939 to catch a glimpse of Their Majesties.

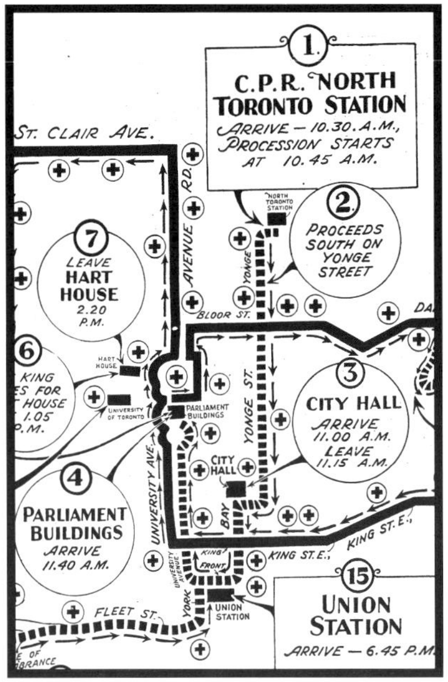

Map of the route through Toronto taken in 1939 showing the part of Yonge travelled by the King and Queen.

Buildings along Yonge Street were festooned with flags and bunting and other decorations. Here we see Simpson's – now The Bay – and the entrance to Eaton's store.

In 1837, the Loyal Volunteers halted the advance of Mackenzie's rebels at College and Yonge. The rebels retreated to Montgomery's Tavern, once at Montgomery and Yonge. There, the Crown forces defeated and dispersed them. Today, a unique monument of the 11-month reign of King Edward VIII (Duke of Windsor) is found on the post office on the site.

Muir Park on Yonge near Lawrence Avenue commemorates Alexander Muir who wrote the song "The Maple Leaf Forever" in 1867, the time of Confederation. The well-known chorus is inscribed on the park masonry:

The Maple Leaf, our emblem dear,
The Maple Leaf forever;
God save our King, and Heaven bless
The Maple Leaf forever.

Edward VII, as Prince of Wales, travelled Yonge Street in 1860. It is appropriate that his royal cypher still decorates the old post office building at Yonge and Charles Streets.

Below: The present Queen, Her Majesty Queen Elizabeth II, and her family have travelled on Ontario's most historic highway. In 1987, the Duke and Duchess of York signed the guest book at the North York Civic Centre on Yonge Street.

Above: At Yonge and Gerrard on the southwest corner is a Toronto-Dominion Bank with bas-relief medallion portraits of Queen Victoria and King Louis XIII carved on the upper facade of the building facing Yonge.

Galbraith Photographs

In 1996 a looseleaf book containing 70 photos of Yonge Street taken in 1922 from Hoggs Hollow in North York to Muloch Drive in Newmarket came into my possession. These photos were taken by a man called Galbraith who was a professional photographer in North York. He apparently was working for the Department of Highways and was commissioned to take pictures of memorable buildings and main intersections from the what was at that time the northern limits of Toronto to Newmarket. An interesting sidelight was that he did not take any photos in Richmond Hill, Aurora, or Newmarket ostensibly because these towns owned and operated the highway right of way in their town and the Ontario Department of Highways did not. I decided that since we were involved in celebrations of the 200 anniversary of the building of Yonge Street that I would go out and photograph the same sites that Galbraith did or as close as I could determine those sites. In addition I also took pictures of main intersections in Richmond Hill, Aurora, Newmarket and Holland Landing since in 1796 Yonge Street was surveyed from Toronto to Holland Landing (the northern terminus is now marked by Anchor Park).

In the next few pages you will see a sampling of these 1922 and 1996 pictures side by side by side. To see the complete set visit the Elman Campbell Museum on Main Street in Newmarket.

Ralph Magel

Top: This picture taken by Galbraith in 1922 was labeled, "Yonge Street looking north from approximately St. Andrews College gate."

Bottom: This view was taken in 1996 looking north on Yonge Street from the North York golf course entrance. Note the underpass of Highway 401 in the upper right corner of the photo.

Above right: is a picture Galbraith in 1922 referred to as "Yonge Street, Brown's store, Lansing."

At the left: is the view of Yonge & Sheppard, looking North, in 1996 after the store, now referred to as Dempsey's Hardware was moved to make way for subway construction.

Above left: is the Dempsey store moved to a new site on Beecroft Road North where it has been refurbished to its early form, with verandah, and is now used as the North York Archives.

Above: In 1922 Galbraith described this view "Yonge Street looking north from Finches corners". Note the tracks to the right. They are part of the Toronto & York Radial Railroad which was taken over by Ontario Hydro in 1922 and run for the next 4 years. This line was finally abandoned in 1948.

Left: Yonge and Finch looking North in 1996. The corner is now dominated by an office building, Xerox, and hi-rise apartments.

Above: This picture was described by Galbraith in 1922 as "G.C. Charlton's store, Newtonbrook."

Right: After some searching this coffee shop was located at the NW corner of Yonge and Drewry W. in North York. The chimney and porch are gone, a small dormer has been added but the windows are correct. Sometimes old houses can go on for a long time.

Above: Is described in 1922 as "Yonge Street looking north at Steeles corners." If you look carefully you can see a Radial car on the line in the lower right corner.

Right: Yonge and Steeles in 1996 has malls, service stations and low rises but a lot more car traffic. Buses have now taken over from the Radial line. Some would be happy to bring it back into operation.

Above: In 1922 Galbraith described this as "Stirling Bank, garage and Victoria Hall, Thornhill." This is the only town north of Toronto in which he took a picture of the downtown.

Right: In 1996 Yonge and Centre Street in Thornhill is a busy intersection with a stop light, the bank is gone but Victoria Hall has become a commercial building.

Galbraith did not take a picture looking south from Richmond Hill but in 1996 a picture taken south from Major Mackenzie Drive shows the nest of high rises all the way to Toronto with the CN Tower piercing the mist above them all.

Above: Galbraith described this as "Yonge Street looking south showing curve on Bond Lake" (note the Radial Car on the siding to the left in the photo just outside of the car barn located behind the trees).

Right: The location as it appears in 1996, the curve has been straightened out, the track is gone, but behind the trees (inset) is the car barn and power house of the former Metropolitan Radial Railroad in sad need of repair.

Many remember with nostalgia the Bond Lake park, which is no more, but was the location for many memorable Sunday picnics in the early part of the century. It was reached by Radial Transit travelling on Yonge Street.

Right: The northernmost picture that Galbraith took was "Yonge Street looking north at Mulock's corner." Note the radial line tracks turning east to cross the fields into downtown Newmarket to continue on to Queensville, Jackson's Point and terminate in Sutton. The Lake Simcoe section of the line was abandoned in 1930 but sections of the right of way north of Newmarket can be still be seen in 1996.

Left: Yonge and Mulock as it appears in 1996 with high-rises on the northeast corner (a bit of the radial right of way can be found behind the building on the NE corner even today). The original Mulock farm and house are still located on the northwest corner with present generation Mulocks still living in it. Most of the farm has been sold to developers who are building a subdivision on the back property.

Above: Galbraith stopped any further pictures at the last one but it is worth noting that in 1996 at the next intersection north, Yonge and Eagle Street, is the seat of government of the Region of York on the northwest corner in a Cardinal architecturally styled building. This building represents one of the most significant buildings on Yonge Street in York Region.

Above: Yonge and Mount Albert Sideroad in Holland Landing is just a few miles south of the upper landing where Augustus Jones ended his survey of Yonge Street for John Graves Simcoe in 1796. Yonge at this point crosses the unfinished lock of the Newmarket Lake Simcoe barge canal. This canal was built in the first decade of 1900 but never saw a barge. The discovery that there would not be enough water to fill the locks, brought the Federal government of the time to defeat.

YONGE STREET CELEBRATIONS

The celebration of the Yonge Street bicentennial was the event that created the material for this book.

A small group of people from the historical societies along Yonge Street primarily in York Region, began planning for the celebrations as early as 1994 with the formation of a 200 Years Yonge Committee. They met to develop an infrastructure to support the celebrations, and finally decided that each town along Yonge Street would develop its plans independently, with a circulation of the information the other societies. When the Region of York became involved through John Scott, the information officer, the groups used the information dispersal facilities of the Region to disseminate information about the events.

Seed money was generated by the sale of 1996 calendars with photo contributions by each town along Yonge Street, as far north as Barrie. The Region of York newspapers owned by Metroland Publishing published a 28 page Yonge street historical supplement, with articles by Terry Carter, in their February 25th, 1996, Sunday edition.

The Ontario Historical Society developed a two-day conference on The Simcoe Legacy: "The Life and times of Yonge Street," which featured speakers describing every aspect of Yonge history.

The Ontario Genealogical Society produced a book *Researching Yonge Street*, containing a series of articles on Yonge Street history. Berchem's second Yonge Street book *Opportunity Road, Yonge Street 1860-1939*, was published.

There was a candlelight walk in Aurora, a display at College Park, a Yonge Street Mall, and the Ontario Trucking Association combined to display the 68 panels which are the basis for this book. At the York Region Administrative Centre in Newmarket a group of actors and descendants of early York Region settlers recreated the handing over by Augustus Jones, surveyor, of the first Yonge Street survey, to John Graves Simcoe. In turn the Lieutenant Governor presented modern Yonge Street documents to Eldred King, chair of the Region of York.

Throughout the spring summer and fall of 1996 events occurred all over Toronto and York Region: parades in North York, Thornhill, Richmond Hill and Newmarket, a giant garage sale on Yonge Street in Aurora, and a canoe re-creation of Simcoe's trip up the West Holland River, through Lake Simcoe and into Penetanguishine. A proclamation traveled down Yonge Street to be signed by officials in the communities along the route. The celebrations ended with the burying of a time capsule at the Regional seat in Newmarket.

Relive those moments through the pictures describing these events, on the following pages.

Ralph Magel

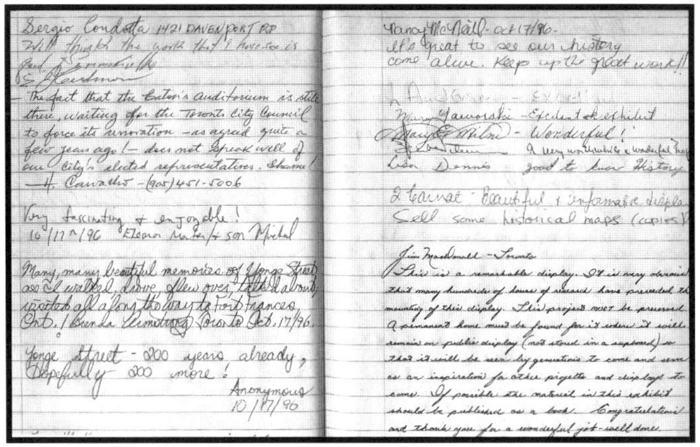

Comments in book with 68 board exhibit, triggered the production of this history.

John Graves Simcoe (actor Woody Lambe) shows original Yonge survey to early settler descendants Paul Millar, Jackie Playter, and Jim Millard during Simcoe Re-creation.

Quaker descendants in Simcoe Re-creation, Sandra Fuller, Sheldon Clark and Jane Zavitts, presented a petition that their ancestors failed to do.

Lorne Smith, left, a descendent of the Berczy settlers, played an axeman in the Simcoe Re-creation ceremonies. He is seen here talking to Augustus Jones, the surveyor, played by John Chappelle.

John Graves Simcoe (actor Woody Lambe) presents a copy of the original Yonge Street survey to Eldred King, Chair of the Region of York, at the Simcoe Re-creation.

"Mr. Yonge Street" Ralph Magel, Newmarket Councillor Gail Parks, and Roy Hamilton from the East Gwillimbury Historical Society display the 200 Years YONGE banner that was destined to grace the Yonge lampposts throughout York Region. (Courtesy the Newmarket Era)

The 200 Years YONGE Committee at their final meeting celebrating chair Mary Lloyd's retirement are left to right: Jaqueline Stuart, Aurora Museum, treasurer; Walter Kent, Innisfil Historical Society; Jane McLaren, Thornhill Society; Mary Lloyd, Richmond Hill Historical Society, chair; Barbara Verney, Bradford West Gwillimbury Historical Society.

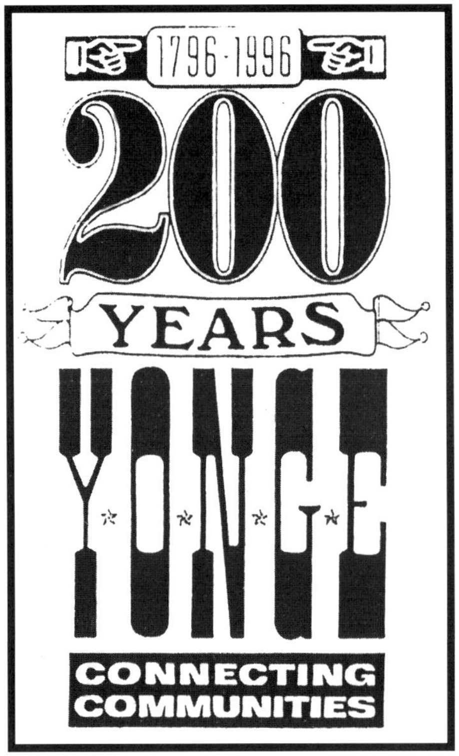

Above: A Yonge Street logo developed by North York graced light standards along that section of the street.

Right: some of the displays mounted by Heritage Toronto, to describe "events", along Yonge Street including one of the earliest and most famous, the MacKenzie Rebellion of 1837.

Above: North York celebrated 200 Years YONGE with a massive parade on Yonge Street in July 1996.

Right: The Chambers of Commerce of York Region struck a coin to commemorate the 200th anniversary of YONGE.

Above: One of the few times Yonge Street has been closed in many years was for the Newmarket Holland Landing Parade.

Left: Some of the 200 vehicles, steam engines and horses that were entered in one of the biggest parades to be seen on Yonge Street in this decade.

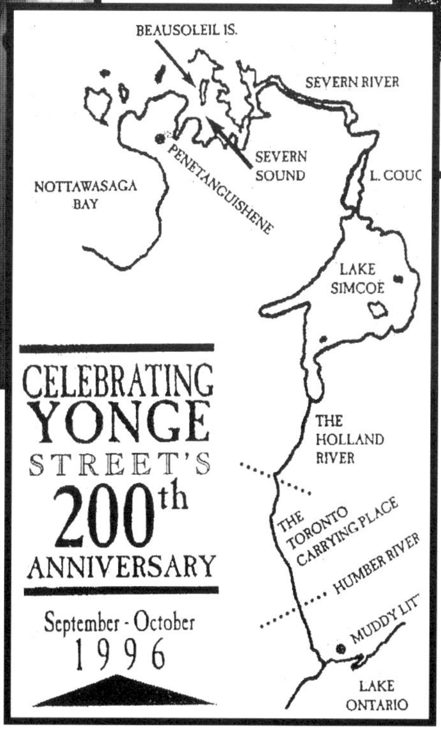

Barbara Verney of the Bradford Historical Society and John Graves Simcoe (actor Michael Stevenson) in 1996 speak at the Bradford East Holland River stop of the canoe re-creation of Simcoe's exploratory trip in approx. 1793. Aian Craig, a Kleinberg teacher (shown in the inset) organized and led the men and women who paddled their canoes up the West Holland River into Lake Simcoe. Over the next few weekends they continued through Lake Simcoe and up the Severn River to Penetanguishine just as Simcoe did before he selected Yonge Street as a portage on his military road to Georgian Bay in 1796.

A proclamation which had begun its travels down Yonge street from Rainy River on Jan. 1, 1996, arrived in York Region in August, to be signed by Eldred King, York Region Chair, and Newmarket Regional Councillor, Tom Taylor.

The proclamation continued its travels down Yonge Street to be handed on from Aurora Mayor Tim Jones, left, and Councillor Ron Wallace, centre, to Vito Spatafora representing Richmond Hill.

In 1997 Jane presented the collection to Chair Eldred King for safekeeping by York Region.

Above left: Jane Beacroft and Margaret Crawford from The Community Heritage Project are shown outside the York Regional Building in 1996 after delivering and setting up the Yonge Street historical displays in the York Hall (above).

Above: Councillor Gail Parks of Newmarket Council conceived the idea that a time capsule containing artifacts from the year 1996 should be buried in a conspicuous spot on Yonge Street. With the help of Glen and Jackie Playter (providing the vault) Armitage Construction (providing the stone) and the Newmarket Lions Cub (providing the plaque), the time capsule was buried on the grounds of the Quaker Meeting House just south of Eagle and Yonge Streets in Newmarket during May of 1997.

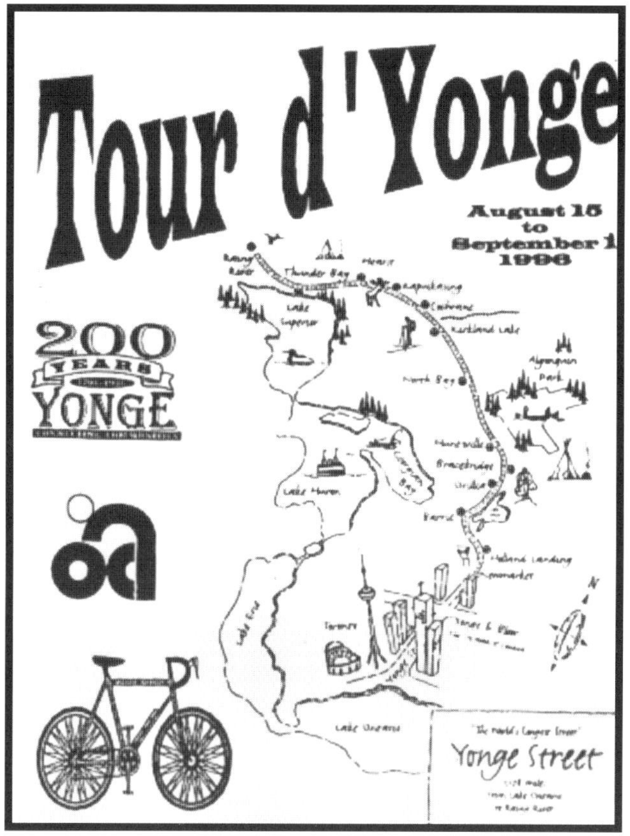

It is only fitting that the final event of the summer consisted of a group of men and women riding bicycles some 1900 kilometres from Rainy River the present terminus of Yonge Street to Toronto where it all started 200 years before. Pauline Whyte and Evelyn Stout of St. Catharines are captured in this Toronto Star photo.

ACKNOWLEDGEMENTS

This publication was made possible by the diligence and dedication of the volunteers, to whom the presentation and promotion of our heritage are labors of love. Their efforts helped make history come alive for the readers of this book and their scholarship has created a legacy worthy of note.

THE YONGE STREET PANELS

The 68 panels that tell the story of Yonge Street were created by the following historical societies and heritage organizations. This project was an integral part of the 200 Years YONGE celebrations and served to put the 1996 events into their historic perspective. (Certain panels which did not pertain particularly to Yonge Street, are marked by ★. They were not used in this book, but are still part of the collection of panels located at the Region of York Administration Building)

- Aurora Museum
- Black Creek Pioneer Village
- Bradford West Gwillimbury Local History Association
- Clans and Scottish Societies of Canada★
- Community History Project
- Dance Collection Danse★
- East Gwillimbury 200 Years Yonge Committee
- German Canadian Heritage Museum
- Grange Historical Society
- Heritage York
- Innisfil Historical Society
- James McCowan Memorial Social History Society★
- La Society d'histoire de Toronto
- Maps Project: Metro Area Heritage Groups

- Mississauga Heritage Foundation*
- Monarchist League of Canada, Metro Toronto Branch
- Newmarket Historical Society
- North Toronto Historical Society
- North York Historical Society
- Ontario Genealogical Society, Toronto Branch
- Ontario Trucking Association
- Ontario Black History Society*
- Richmond Hill Public Library
- Rousseau Project/Le Project Rousseau
- Society of Heritage Associates
- Toronto Field Naturalists
- Town of York Historical Society
- United Empire Loyalists, Toronto Branch

The original typing was done by Mavis MacDonald and the panels' typesetting was by Clifford Collier, courtesy of the Ontario Genealogical Society. The scanning of the images for the book was done by Paul Millard and Ralph Magel of the Newmarket Historical Society.

The panels were "snapshots" of individual topics, rather than exhaustive treatments of the subjects. In the same way, not all of the materials available on the panels could be included in this publication. If we have whetted your appetite for more information on a particular subject, we would encourage you to contact – or join – the organizations which created the materials. Please refer to the Sources and References section on Page 142 to see where we obtained the material used on specific pages in this book.

Material for this publication was provided by volunteers from the Toronto Branch of the Ontario Genealogical Society (OGS). The OGS was founded to collect genealogical and historical data, to assist members in their study of genealogical research and to issue genealogical publications, especially relating to Ontario. It was organized in 1961 and received its Ontario charter in 1967. Toronto Branch maintains a database of all known places of worhsip and related registers in historic York County as well as known cemetery locations and transcribed marker inscriptions. Donations in material and time are welcome.

Toronto Branch, OGS, Box 518, Station K., Toronto ON M4P 2G9

ACKNOWLEDGEMENTS

THE GALBRAITH PHOTOS

This remarkable set of photographs was commissioned by the Ontario Government's Department of Highways in 1922. The photographer, Alexander Galbraith, traveled much of the original section of Yonge Street, capturing streetscapes and notable buildings.

A collection of these photographs was presented to Newmarket historian Ralph Magel, who saw in them the opportunity for a more modern, yet still historic, presentation of Yonge Street's story. By matching the originals to current settings and juxtaposing the photographs, he has created a "Then and Now" record that seemed quite appropriate within the covers of this book.

The publishers gratefully acknowledge the time and efforts that various contributors have made to this project, in particular the organizations which did the research and compiling of the original Yonge Street Historical Panels. For those interested in pursuing historical research, we would recommend that you contact the specific organizations who contributed the materials. Credits for these materials are listed on Page 136.

While we have attempted to gain permission and to acknowledge the source of all materials used in the production of this book, we apologize in advance for any errors or oversights that may have occurred in this regard. Please contact the publishers so that all appropriate changes may be made in subsequent editions.

Thanks are expressed to the Archives of Ontario, Christine Bourolias, Reference Archivist, Carolyn Gray, Senior Archivist, The Baldwin Room of the Toronto Reference Library for the use of pictures used in this publication.

BIBLIOGRAPHY

It is beyond the scope of this section of the book to describe all the references that the various organizations consulted for their particular section. But it is worthwhile to point out some of the reference books and news articles that came out in relation to the 200 Years YONGE.

East Gwillimbury in the Nineteenth Century by Gladys M. Rolling

Elizabeth Postuma Simcoe 1762 - 1852 a biography by Mary Beacock Fryer, Dundurn Press 1989

Great Canadian Road by Jan Myers, Red Rock Publishing Co. Ltd. 1977

North Toronto by Don Ritchie, Boston Mills Press, Book Research by Whitchurch History Book Committee - 1993

Opportunity Road Yonge Street 1860-1939 F. R. Berchem, published by Natural Heritage 1996

The Quakers in Canada - a History by Arthur G. Dorland, 1968, The Ryerson Press

The Visible Past - The pictorial history of Simcoe County by Adelaid Leith, published by County of Simcoe, Ontario, Canada. 1992

Whitchurch Township Research by Whitchurch History Book Committee, 1993

Researching Yonge Street by Ontario Genealogical Society, Toronto Branch, 1996

York Pioneer 1996 Volume 9 pg 32 Yonge Street 200 article

Yonge Street Story 1793-1860 by F.R. Bercham published by Natural Heritage, 1996

Toronto Star articles Feb. 11,12,13, 1996; Feb. 28, 1996; March 16, 1996; June 7, 1996; June 8, 1996; June 9, 1996;April 29, 1996; June 29, 1996; June 30, 1996; July 1, 1995;July 2, 1996, July 3, 1996; September 14, 1996.

Toronto Sun articles March 10, 1996; Feb. 18, 1996; July 28, 1996.

The Globe & Mail article April 27, 1996.

The Newmarket Aurora Era/Banner, Richmond Hill Liberal, articles in supplement Sunday Feb 25, 1996.

INDEX

SOURCES & REFERENCES

Cover Pictures: Left to Right
St. John's Anglican (York Mills)
Modern streetscape - Yonge and Finch - Newmarket Historical Society
Quaker Meeting House - Newmarket Historical Society
Centre streetscape - Yonge early 1900s - Aurora Historical Society
John Graves Simcoe - Ontario Archives
recent streetscape - Yonge in 1940's - Aurora Historical Society
Region of York building - Region of York Archives

PHOTO CREDITS

Pg. 3 Mr. Eldred King - Chairman, Region of York - Region of York Archives

Pg. 4 - National Archives - NMC47968

Pg. 5 - St. John's House – National Archives - NMC47968; Survey Map - National Archives

Pg. 7 - Toronto Carrying Place Map, First Nations' Trail - The Rosseau Project

Pg. 8 - portrait - unknown- The Rosseau Project

Pg. 9 - Globe & Mail article, Thursday Nov. 12, 1967

Pg. 11 - Early French Map - La Societe d'histoire de Toronto – National Archives

Pg. 12 - Fort Rouille - La Societe d'histoire de Toronto - National Archives

Pg. 13 - Etienne Brule - La Societe d'histoire de Toronto - National Archives

Pg. 14 - Augustus Jones surveyor, rotogravure - National Archives Survey map - OGST Ontario Genealogical Society Toronto Branch

Pg. 15 - Ambrotype portrait of Augustus Jones courtesy of AOLS Archives

Pg. 15 - Genealogy Charts - OGST

Pg. 16 - portrait William Moll Berczy - GCHM - German Canadian Heritage Museum sketch - Public Archives of Canada

Pg. 17 - painting - GCHM

Pg. 18 - map - Miles 1878 Atlas

Pg. 19 - OGST Township Papers for York , Archives of Ontario RG1 C-IV Box 209, envelope 552-1 microfilm MS 658-5330

Pg. 20 - Map courtesy Toronto Registry Office

Pg. 23 - logos - C. W. Jefferys Collection - National Archives of Canada; Vanderburgh House - Richmond Hill Historical Society UELT

Pg. 25 - Map courtesy Toronto Registry Office.

Pg. 26 - BCPV - Black Creek Pioneer Village

Pg. 27 - BCPV - Black Creek Pioneer Village

Pg. 28 - Road and communications from York to Nottawasaga Bay, W. Chewett, [1794]; B-34; Archives of Ontario; AO 3046

Pg. 29 - Sketch map of Upper Canada showing the routes Lt. Gov. Simcoe took on journeys, [1795] Simcoe family Fonds; F 47-5-1-037; Archives of Ontario; AO 1092

Pg. 30 - Painting of Lieutenant John Graves Simcoe from Metropolitan Toronto Reference Library

Pg. 31 - Sketch from CHP Canadian History Project files

Pg. 32 - Sketches from CHP files

Pg. 33 - Sketches from CHP files

Pg. 34 - Photos from OTA Ontario Trucking Association

Pg. 35 - Photos from OTA

Pg. 36 - Sketches & Proclamations from CHP

Pg. 37 - Photos & sketches from CHP & Baldwin Room at the Metropolitan Reference Library

Pg. 38 - Map from CHP, Goad Atlas, 1808 Fire Insurance Plans

Pg. 39 - Photos & drawing from CHP files

Pg. 40 - Photos & map from CHP files

Pg. 41 - Photos & map from CHP files

Pg. 42 - Maps from HY Heritage York, Tremayne 1860 Map

Pg. 43 - Photos from HY

Pg. 43 - Photos from HY

Pg. 44 - Photos from HY

Pg. 45 - Photos from HY

Pg. 46 - City of Toronto Archives

Pg. 46 - Photos from NTHS North Toronto Historical Societ

Pg. 47 - Photo from NTHS

Pg. 48 - Photo from NTHS

Pg. 48 - Atkinson Family

Pg. 49 - Photo from NTHS

Pg. 49 - Consumers Gas

Pg. 50 - Photos from NYHS North York Historical Society

Pg. 50 - Willowdale photograph from Dept. of Highways - Galbraith

Pg. 51 - Newtonbrook photograph from Dept. of Highways - Galbraith

Pg. 51 - Photos from NYHS

Pg. 52 - Photos from NYHS

Pg. 53 - Photos from NYHS

Pg. 54 - Photos from RHPL Richmond Hill Public Library

Pg. 55 - Photos from RHPL

Pg. 56 - Photos from AHS Aurora Historical Society

Pg. 57 - Photos from AHS

Pg. 58/59 - Photos from AHS

Pg. 60/61 - Photos from NHS Newmarket Historical Society

Pg. 60/61 - Line drawings by George Leusby

Pg. 62/63 - Photos from NHS

Pg. 64/65 - Photos from NHS

Pg. 66/67 - Photos from EG200YYC East Gwillimbury 200 Years Yonge Committee

Pg. 68/69 - Photos from EG200YYC

Pg. 70/71 - Photos from BWGLHA Bradford West Gwillimbury Local History Association

Pg. 72/73 - Photos from BWGLH

Pg. 74/75 - Photos from IHS Innisfil Historical Society

Pg. 76/77 - Photos from IHS

Pg. 78/79 - Photos from CHP

Pg. 80/81 - Photos from NH Natural Heritage

Pg. 82/83 - Photos from GHS Grange Historical Society

Pg. 84/85 - Photos from GHS

Pg. 86/87 - Photos from GHS Jefferys collection Picture Gallery of Canadian History ISBN 0-07-077704-7Pg. 88/89 - Photos from CHP Jefferys collection Picture Gallery of Canadian History ISBN 0-07-077704-7

Pg. 90/91 - Photos from CHP

Pg. 92/99- Church Photos from OGST Ontario Genealogical Society Toronto Branch volunteers (old photos from Robertson's Landmarks of Toronto 1904 republished from Toronto "Evening Telegram")

Pg. 100/107 - Cemetery Photos from OGST volunteers & as above from Robertson's Landmarks of Toronto

Pg. 108/109 - from files of SHS The Society of Heritage Associates

Pg. 110/113 - from files Monarchist League of Canada, Metro Toronto Branch

Pg. 114/125 - from copies of pictures photographed by Alexander W. Galbraith (1867-1950) in 1922 for the Department of Highways and originals by Ralph Magel in 1996

Pg. 126/135 - Photos by Ralph Magel, Newmarket Historical Society, in 1996

Published by Natural Heritage/Natural History Inc.
P.O. Box 95, Station O, Toronto, Ontario M4A 2M8

Second Edition
Printed and bound in Canada by Hignell Printing Limited

Back Cover Photos: *Top left:* Yonge Street looking South from York Mills Hotel, 1922. *Bottom left:* Yonge Street looking south from Jolly Miller Hotel, North York, Toronto, 1996. *Top middle:* Yonge Street looking north, Thornhill, 1922. *Bottom middle:* Yonge and Centre Street looking North, Thornhill, 1996. *Top right:* Yonge Street looking north from Elgin Mills, 1922. *Bottom right:* Yonge and Elgin Mills looking north, Richmond Hill, 1996.
1922 photos by Alexander Galbraith. 1996 photos by Ralph Magel.

Canadian Cataloguing in Publication Data

200 years Yonge; a history

Includes bibliographical references and index.
ISBN 1-896219-49-7

1. Yonge Street (Toronto : Ont.) - History. 2. Toronto (Ont.) - History. 3. York (Ont. : Regional municipality) - History. 4. Simcoe (Ont. : County) - History. I. Magel, Ralph. II. Title: Two hundred years Yonge.

FC3097.67.T86 1998 971.3'54 C98-932771-X
F1059.5.T6875Y65 1998

The Canada Council for the Arts since 1957 | Le Conseil des Arts du Canada depuis 1957

Natural Heritage/Natural History Inc. acknowledges the support received for its publishing program from the Canada Council Block Grant Program. We also acknowledge with gratitude the assistance of the Association for the Export of Canadian Books, Ottawa.